Theology Today
17 The Theology of Grace

Theology Today

GENERAL EDITOR:

EDWARD YARNOLD, S.J.

No. 17

The Theology of Grace

BY

CORNELIUS ERNST, O.P.

FIDES PUBLISHERS, INC.

NOTRE DAME, INDIANA

ISBN 0 8190–0544–4

Nihil Obstat:
Mgr. F. G. Thomas, S.T.L.
15th June 1973

Imprimatur:
Mgr. D. Leonard, V.G.
15th June 1973

Printed in Great Britain

CONTENTS

FOREWORD

Some readers may prefer to begin with a brief look at chapter 3, and then perhaps return to it after the first two chapters.

Scriptural quotations generally follow the Revised Standard Version, copyrighted 1946 and 1952 by the Division of Christian Education of the National Council of Churches in the USA and used by permission, although I have occasionally modified the translation slightly. Other translations are my own, unless otherwise indicated. As far as possible, any writings mentioned in the book are listed at the end in the Suggestions for Further Reading, when they are available in English.

This little book is dedicated to Ignace D'hert O.P., who is responsible for more of it than he would perhaps care to admit.

Cornelius Ernst O.P.

ABBREVIATIONS

PG   Patrologia Graeca
PL   Patrologia Latina

CHAPTER ONE

THE LANGUAGE OF GRACE

Our English word 'grace' translates the Latin *gratia*, which in turn translates the Greek *charis* of the New Testament. The continuity of meaning suggested by speaking of 'translation' is real, but very much more complex than might at first appear. Each word had and still has its appropriate contexts and ranges of use, so that we have to see the continuity as one of overlapping areas rather than as a single straight line, or indeed a single point.

As far as the English 'grace' is concerned it is probably true that there is very little interplay between its theological and its secular uses. We do not ordinarily in a theological context have in mind, say, the poise of the gymnast or the ballet dancer, and when upon occasion the connexion is in fact made, it may surprise us pleasantly for a moment without contributing anything very permanent to our general theological understanding. For instance, Gerard Manley Hopkins speaks of 'God's better beauty, grace' in the poem 'To what serves mortal beauty?', but it can hardly be said that the connexion made here has influenced our ordinary theological usage.

It might indeed be argued that the interplay of theological and secular senses of the English word would be inappropriate. New Testament usage hardly ever makes a connexion between *charis* and what might be called an aesthetic quality, although such a connexion might have been invited by secular Greek usage. This theological problem – whether it is appropriate or desirable to extend the use of a traditional theological term by allowing it to assume other usages which it might have

11

in secular contexts not envisaged in its original biblical context – is a difficult one and may be set aside at least for the moment. It is enough to note that the Greek, Latin and English words have had different histories, even though at all times a more or less consistent attempt has been made in theological contexts to regulate the use of the term in the European languages by the use of the term *charis* in the New Testament.

A failure to recognize the historical or 'diachronic' character of linguistic meaning has unfortunately led to a great deal of fairly sterile dispute. As far as grace is concerned, Roman Catholics and Protestants were for centuries and perhaps still are divided not only by distinctive usages of the word 'grace' (or its European equivalents) but also by the claim that the distinctive usage in each case more accurately represents the New Testament meaning of *charis*. What is quite undeniable is that a shift in the theological meaning of *gratia* took place in Latin scholastic theology towards the end of the twelfth and the early part of the thirteenth century. In an early work, St Thomas Aquinas writes:

> Thus if we were to speak of God's grace not as some habitual gift but as God's very mercy itself . . . man cannot perform any good work without God's grace. But in the mode of speech common today people use the word 'grace' for a habitual justifying gift (*Quaestio disputata de Veritate*, 24,14).

St Thomas was clearly aware that changes in the use of the word *gratia* had occurred; it was something he had to take account of as a theologian who, especially in the theology of grace, had to reflect on the writings of St Augustine, the 'Doctor of Grace'.

Now as a matter of fact the difference in usage to which he draws attention is very similar to that which has divided Roman Catholic and Protestant theology; unfortunately the recognition that changes in linguistic usage occur, and must occur, without necessarily involving theological betrayal, has not been easily avail-

12

able to theologians of either confession. Further, it would be misleading to suggest that theological differences were 'merely linguistic', if by this phrase it was understood that the use of a good dictionary would have sorted things out. The differences of linguistic usage were the expression of very different styles of theological procedure and of total theological comprehension; but mutual understanding might have been reached more readily if the historical dimension of theological reflection had been more generally recognized.

It might then seem appropriate to begin this brief study of the theology of grace by looking at the use of *charis* in the New Testament. We need not suppose that our findings, provisional and tentative as they must in any case be, necessarily provide an ultimate criterion by which to assess the truth and validity of any theology of grace. For instance, it may well be that if we review the history of the theology of grace we may come to the conclusion that such a theology may usefully include elements not explicitly envisaged in New Testament usage. Theology is not just the repetition of biblical words. But however this may be, it is undeniable that any theology of grace must take account of the New Testament usage of *charis*.

Now what we first notice when we review the use of *charis* in the New Testament is that it is dominantly a Pauline word, occurring perhaps 100 times in the Pauline epistles (excluding Hebrews) and perhaps fifty times altogether in the rest of the New Testament. These figures are sufficiently massive to be impressive, and any attempt to refine the statistics would raise more problems than it would solve. The figures, taken in this global way, show that while nearly all the New Testament writers make occasional use of the word *charis*, Paul (together perhaps with writers influenced by him) makes a distinctively large use of the word. This is far from saying that Paul has a 'theology' of *charis*. All that the statistics show is that when Paul preaches his gospel his personal vocabulary includes a notably extensive use of a word which is also part of the general New Testament vocabulary. What we should expect, then, is that his use of *charis* is associated with distinctively Pauline themes, those which taken together might be said to be the themes of his 'theology', the themes he develops in the preaching of his gospel.

This point is of sufficiently general importance, perhaps, to be put in different terms. It is at least arguable that Grace did not become a distinct theological theme, the focus of theological reflection, till the later writings of St Augustine, in his controversy with Pelagius and his followers; before this controversy, as we shall see, Augustine could discuss topics which he himself later considered or we ourselves might now consider to belong to the theology of grace, without any distinctive use of the word *gratia*. It is important, especially when we propose in a book like this to study the 'theology of grace', not to be led by our own preoccupations into finding explicit treatment of theological themes where there may be only a more or less differentiated context, a web of associations. It seems to me that for St Paul, *charis* belongs to a web of associations, perhaps as a point at which associations cluster thickly, rather than to the group of themes of reflection or preaching or dispute, the implications of which he explores and to some extent systematizes, such as, say, justification. If we were able to ask him what he meant by *charis*, it seems to me that he would need to pause and *reconstruct* his use of the word, in a way not unlike the way in which we should have to try and do it for him; and we should not be surprised to find that the different uses of the word in particular contexts were only loosely associated. One question we shall have to ask ourselves later in this book is whether it is desirable to try to construct a theology of grace at all.

'Grace' (= *charis*) occurs in nearly every greeting at

the beginning and at the end of Paul's letters, frequently in combination with 'peace'. The ordinary Jewish practice was to wish 'peace', *shalom*, the blessing of God; the corresponding Greek practice took the form of the salutation *chaire* = Latin *salve*, which is usually rendered by our 'Hail', cognate with the German *Heil*, health and salvation; compare the greeting to our Lady, Lk 1.28, where there is a play on the word *chaire*, 'hail', and the Greek for 'favoured one', *kecharitomene*. The similarity of sound between *chaire* and *charis* may have helped Paul to combine Hebrew and Greek formulae into a distinctive formulation of his own. His formulation frequently has a solemnity with the overtones of a liturgical blessing, and is ordinarily attached, at the end of his letters particularly, to Jesus Christ. The fullest expression of this solemn benediction is to be found in 2 Cor 13.14, 'The grace of our Lord Jesus Christ and the love of God and fellowship of the Holy Spirit be with you all,' a text since used frequently in Christian liturgies. Paul's letters, we should remember, would presumably have been read aloud at Christian assemblies, and the formulae of greeting and farewell may be seen as blessings bestowed by an apostle on a Christian community. These communities would in general be familiar with the so-called 'Aaronic blessing', used in both synagogue and Temple:

> The Lord bless you and keep you:
> The Lord make his face to shine upon you,
>   and be gracious to you:
> The Lord lift up his countenance upon you,
>   and give you peace (Num 6.24-26).

Certainly associated with this use of 'grace' in Paul's greetings is the more general use of the word in the rest of the New Testament. Very summarily, this general sense of 'grace' is more or less equivalent to 'kindness', 'favour', especially as shown in action, nearly always the benevolence or beneficence of God. Behind this New Testament usage is the Old Testa-

15

ment, where the Greek of the Septuagint version regularly translates the Hebrew *hen* by *charis*. In accordance with the whole texture of Hebrew awareness of God, God's favour is sensed as a community of feeling between God and man, a sympathy or compassion. We may take as an example here the wonderful passage, Ex 33.12-23, with its association of the themes of favour and mercy, God's sovereign elective purpose, the mutual knowledge by personal name of God and his people, God's face and presence and the hidden transcendence of his glory:

> And the Lord said to Moses, 'This very thing that you have spoken I will do; for you have found favour in my sight, and I know you by name.' Moses said, 'I pray thee, show me thy glory.' And he said, 'I will make all my goodness pass before you, and will proclaim before you my name "The Lord"; and I will be gracious to whom I will be gracious, and will show mercy on whom I will show mercy. But,' he said, 'you cannot see my face; for man shall not see me and live' (verses 17-20).

It cannot of course be assumed that these associations are all actively present when 'grace' occurs anywhere in the New Testament; we must always consider the context of the occurrence, and assess with what degree of poetic pregnancy the language in each case is being charged. But the associations are in fact there in the Biblical tradition to be evoked; and it is Paul among the New Testament writers who most richly orchestrates his gospel of Jesus Christ with these associations.

Paul made his rediscovery of these associations through a personal experience of the living God in the risen Jesus; it is, I think, impossible to read his letters without a sense of this immediate experience which sustains all he writes. 'But when he who had set me apart before I was born, and had called me through his grace, was pleased to reveal his Son to [or in] me, in order that I might preach him among the Gentiles,

16

I did not confer with flesh and blood . . .' (Gal 1.15-16).
Paul has just been describing his own zealous practice
of Judaism; and the purpose of the text we have
quoted is at least in part to set within a larger order of
continuity of divine purpose the violent discontinuity
in his own personal life between his previous practice
of Judaism and his present preaching of the gospel of
Jesus Christ. It is characteristic that he should establish
this continuity in the terms of the calling of the
prophet Jeremiah (Jer 1.4 f.). A great deal in Paul's
letters, especially Galatians and Romans, is concerned
to show that turning to the risen Jesus is a returning
to the living God of the 'Scriptures', i.e. the Old Testament, behind and beyond the legalistic structures
within which the scriptural revelation had been con-
strained by post-biblical Jewish tradition. Paul's personal experience became the key to his understanding
of the purposes of God, as his experience itself found
expression in the language of those whom he felt
to be his true predecessors as servants of the living
God.

If we take as a single exegetical unit the undoubtedly
Pauline letters (Thessalonians, Corinthians, Galatians,
Philippians, Romans), it is possible to see a certain
development in Paul's use of 'grace', which then takes
a rather different turn in the letters to the Colossians
and Ephesians. We may suppose that the demands
made on him by the preaching and defence of his
gospel led to a special emphasis on God's mode of
action in justification, so that in Romans, the most
coherent account of his gospel, the word occurs very
frequently. The general background of his use of the
word we may see in the formulas of greeting and farewell. There then occur certain sharply particularized
uses of the word *charis*, some of which are not easy to
render in English. One such expression is 'the grace
given to me' (e.g. 1 Cor 3.10), where Paul is always
thinking of his apostolic calling and commission (cf.
Gal 1.15-16; 2.9; 1 Cor 15.10; Rom 1.4; 12.3, 15.15).

What is distinctive about the use of *charis* in these cases is that God's benevolence is both personalized in Paul and directed to the particular function of preaching the gospel to the Gentiles: God's grace is both to him and works through him. In the formulas of blessing, God's grace is invoked upon the community, and is not specified in any distinctive way.

Another instance of the particularizing use of *charis*, where the English translations usually avoid the word 'grace', is Paul's application of the word to the collection he was making among the Gentile churches for the poor in Jerusalem (1 Cor 16.3; 2 Cor 8.1, 4, 6, 7, 19). We may not suppose that this particularized use of the word was totally dissociated in Paul's mind from a broader theological use, because in the very same chapter of 2 Corinthians where he is discussing the collection, he points to the example of Jesus: 'For you know the grace of our Lord Jesus Christ, that though he was rich, yet for your sake he became poor, so that by his poverty you might become rich' (8.9). Both in the case of the community among whom the collection is being made and in the case of Jesus himself, God's free giving of himself in grace is particularized, embodied and manifested in an action, where human compassion is shown by self-deprivation on behalf of another. The example of Jesus, here called a *charis* or grace, is of course most powerfully set out in the hymn of Philippians 2.6-11, in the context of a recommendation to selflessness.

Chapter 8 of 2 Corinthians also illustrates another association of the word *charis* which only appears in English as 'thanks' (v. 16, 'thanks be to God'). Again, we should be careful not to dismiss this connection as merely verbal; it re-appears at a highly significant moment in Romans 7.24-5: 'Who will deliver me from this body of death? Thanks (*charis*) be to God through Jesus Christ our Lord', where the expression of gratitude pregnantly includes an allusion to the gift for which thanks are being given. Paul likes to associate

18

charis with *eucharistia,* thanksgiving, e.g. 1 Cor 1.4; 2 Cor 4.15.

These examples (and many more could be provided) should be enough to show that Paul did not use the word we translate 'grace' as a sharply-defined concept, with a concern for theological consistency. We might say that he used it poetically, meaning that under the pressure of powerful enthusiastic feeling the word excited associations and even perhaps created them when Paul set about preaching the gospel of God's transcendent generosity to man in Jesus Christ. It is important to bear this in mind when we examine Paul's use of the word in the more systematic exposition of his gospel in Romans; for it would be a mistake, I believe, to try to pin down his meaning even there to any more or less philosophical category, whether the categories are taken from Aristotle (as has been common in the Roman Catholic tradition) or have a more or less 'existential' ring (e.g. 'event', 'action', 'situation', as in some modern German Protestant writers). It does not seem to me that even in Romans Paul is talking *about* grace in the same way as he talks *about* God, man, Jesus, or even the Law or baptism. To understand Paul's use of 'grace' we have to try to reconstitute an experience, not to analyse an idea.

In Romans Paul continues to use *charis* in the different ways we have already noticed, though when he speaks of the collection for Jerusalem (15.25 f.) he uses other religiously coloured words instead. But we soon begin to realize that he is now using the word more constructively, often in the polarity of an opposition or supported by some word of similar meaning. Thus at the keypoint of the letter, after showing that both Gentile and Jew have sinned and are alienated from God, he goes on: 'They are justified as a gift by his grace through the redemption which is in Christ Jesus' (3.24). 'As a gift' translates an adverbial expression which amplifies and emphasizes the sense of 'grace', also of course part of an adverbial expression.

19

What Paul is talking *about* is God's justifying action and its means, redemption in Jesus Christ; the adverbial expressions indicate the mode of this action, its undeserved generosity in regard to sinful humanity. 'Grace' is neither a sort of secondary agent or the instrument of God's action; just as 'as a gift' might be translated 'freely', 'undeservedly', so too 'by his grace' might be translated 'graciously', 'gratuitously'.

What might seem a purely grammatical point may be insisted upon by a comparison. When I say I have something 'in my mind', I do not mean that the mind is a sort of receptacle (perhaps rather like the brain) in which items of information are stored – though modern talk about computers makes this seem more plausible; I mean merely that I intend to do such and such, or that I want to talk about such and such. We should not suppose that adverbial expressions using 'by' or 'in' must always be construed in the primary instrumental or local senses of the prepositions.

Two more uses of *charis* with prepositions in adverbial expressions may be examined with the discussion above in mind. In chapter 4, Paul is discussing the case of Abraham and the way in which his faith was accounted justification. He says: 'Now in the case of one who performs works, his reward is not reckoned as a matter of grace but as a matter of due' (v.4). What I have clumsily translated by 'as a matter of' represents the single preposition *kata* (= Latin *secundum*). The polar opposition 'grace/due' helps to sharpen the sense of 'grace'; but again the adverbial expression needs to be taken as a whole, as qualifying the entire relationship. Later in the same chapter, continuing the argument which opposes Abraham's faith to the works of the Law, Paul says with untranslatable brevity: 'The reason why (the promised inheritance in Abraham rests) on faith is that (it may be) a matter of grace' (v.16), again using the preposition *kata*, again then qualifying the whole mode of the relationship God seeks and establishes in justification. Here 'grace' and 'faith' are seen as correlatives, though neither should be taken in isolation as somehow 'psychological' characteristics.

Perhaps at this point we should stand back from Paul's involved argumentation and try to feel our way into the overmastering pressure of his concern. We might say that what Paul is trying to communicate is his dominating conviction about the mode of God's dealings with men: the way in which those dealings have been in one way or another misunderstood, above all in the Jewish religion which specially prided itself on its insight into God's purposes; and the way in which if one looks closely enough into the past, above all the past seen in the light of God's supreme revelation of his purposes in the death and resurrection of Jesus Christ, then a deep continuity is disclosed, deeper than the apparent discontinuity between the fact of Jesus and contemporary Jewish religion (a discontinuity vividly experienced by Paul in his own conversion). We could try to sum up what Paul so intensely perceives by saying that all God's dealings with men are the expression of an unrestrained and sovereign generosity of self-giving, seeking an unrestrained self-surrender in response, so that God and man can meet – as they can only meet – in the freedom and the communion of mutual gift and self-giving. Jewish religion had tried to safeguard God's transcendent sovereignty by making what was only an intermediary, the Law, into the irrefragable and uninfringible embodiment of God's demand; Paul sees that God's sovereignty is above all, first and last, a supreme sovereignty of *grace*, of incomprehensible free self-giving, seeking a communion of self-surrender in love, *agape*. No matter what human purposes may be, they all run astray if they do not spring from that fine point and origin of freedom which can only be touched, at the quick of man, by an initiative and an appeal, a calling, which asks only for the whole of man in a self-giving which stirs that very quick into a new being, by a new

21

birth: 'Through the law I died to the law so as to live to God. I was crucified together with Christ; but I am alive, yet it is no longer I, it is Christ who lives in me' (Gal 2.19-20). It is now Christ crucified who is the supreme embodiment of God's sovereign purpose of grace, not the law as the embodiment of God's sovereign demand: Christ the Son whom God did not spare (Rom 8.32), Christ who emptied himself and took the form of a servant (Phil 2.7 f.) so that we might live with him (Rom 6.8) by his Spirit to cry 'Abba, Father' (Rom 8.15). Surrendering ourselves in faith to God, above all in baptism (Rom 6.3 f.), we surrender ourselves to the manifest embodiment of his purposes in the death and resurrection of Jesus Christ, and by surrendering share in that death and resurrection, becoming conformed to his image (Rom 8.29) in the obedience of his surrender to his Father. The adverbial expressions containing the word 'grace' are an attempt to characterize the unique mode of this single and yet differentiated manifestation of God's incomprehensible generosity.

This somewhat impressionistic attempt to lay bare the nerve of Paul's gospel may help us to understand those other uses of *charis* in Romans where it does not appear in adverbial expressions with a preposition but as the grammatical and even logical subject of a statement. Again we must remind ourselves that we are dealing, even in Romans, with thought in intense and excited motion, not with the cool deliberations of an analytic theologian.

Having firmly established the principle that the peace of right relationship with God is his gift to the surrender of faith, Paul goes on in chapter 5 of Romans to supply a parallel expression for this peace: it is the *grace* in which we have come to stand by way of Jesus, exulting in the assurance of God's glory to become manifest to and in us (vv.1-2). Now this may remind us of the 'state of grace' of later theology and catechisms; but one point at least in Paul's account ought to give us pause. He is speaking in the first person *plural*, and the 'we' is not merely a sum of individuals. Paul is talking about something shared, something entered into in common through Jesus Christ, a blessedness of peace with God after alienation. We would do better not to try to define his meaning more closely until we have looked further ahead in this chapter. Paul goes on to describe the ground of our exultation and assurance: it is the Spirit of God's love for us and ours for him poured out in our hearts (v.5, a favourite text of St Augustine's); and it is the visible manifestation of that incomprehensible love in the death of Jesus (love, *agape*, in both verses 5 and 8). The death of Jesus is the expression of God's reconciling love, and so is the ground of our exultation and our hope of total salvation and transformation into the glory of God (cf. verses 9-11, and 1 Cor 15.2 f., 2 Cor 3.17-18 for 'glory').

What follows now is a tense account of conflict, projected as a drama, in which sin, death and grace play their distinctive parts. It would be going too far to call Paul's use of these terms 'personification'; perhaps we may say that he represents sin, death and grace, imaginatively and rhetorically, as 'forces' or 'powers' – compare, for instance, an old-fashioned patriot's use of 'England' or a politician's use of 'capitalism'. The field of action of these forces, the body on which they are at work, is mankind, humanity as a whole, polarized in two representative men, each the progenitor of alternative stems of mankind – Adam and Jesus, who is called in 1 Cor 15.45 the last or ultimate Adam. (Compare modern talk about Eastern and Western 'blocs'.) Mankind is seen as a single historical corporate humanity; yet there has been a critical turning-point in the history which allows for polarization, attraction into one or another field of force. One field of force is dominated by sin and death, the other by grace; one history is initiated by a deliberate transgression, the other by a gift, a grace bestowed (*charisma*). But Paul has to guard against a simple dualistic parallelism: the field of force of grace is immeasurably superior to the field of force of sin and death. Grace unifies, sin disperses; sin masters, grace gives mastery with and through Jesus Christ, bestows the eternal life of the new aeon which has conquered death.

What I have tried to do in this account is to suggest the way in which Paul's language is working by introducing metaphors which are not his own but which might seem to work in a similar way. My account needs to be carefully compared with Paul's own, and modified accordingly. But if my account has been even partially successful, it should be clear that Paul is using 'grace' to talk about a realm, a regime, an economy or dispensation, which in principle embraces all mankind, the whole of humanity in its historical course ('the many' is a Hebraism for 'all'). 'Grace' is that order which is initiated by the sovereign generosity of God's self-giving manifested in the death and resurrection of Jesus Christ. It seems to me that if we read Paul attentively and try to understand him in his own terms, our understanding will express itself in a language of metaphor, arising out of a newly-discovered sense of the solidarity of human kind, a solidarity of alienation and despair and a solidarity of liberation and life. It is such a solidarity that Paul tries to represent when he talks about the 'body' of redeemed humanity, even in this first group of letters (1 Cor 12.12 f.; Rom 12.3 f.), which is why the word 'body' was slipped into my account. It may very well be that we should want to go further, and try to express our understanding of Paul's vision in the language of a systematic view of the world; but we must, I believe, *begin* by an effort of imaginative sympathy.

It is in the New Testament itself, indeed in the letters traditionally attributed to Paul as author, that we find such an effort to present a Pauline vision of

24

the order of grace in the context of a total view of the world. Without entering into the complex problems of authorship here, I shall merely say that I am attracted by the view of the most recent full-length commentary on Ephesians, by the German Roman Catholic J. Gnilka, that this letter is the work of a Pauline 'school' which grew up round the Apostle in the course of his long stay at Ephesus. What is at any rate clear is that Ephesians (and Colossians) differ from the earlier letters not so much in their 'content' as in their perspectives. While the perspective of the earlier letters might be called *historical*, the perspective of these later letters might be called *cosmic*. In the earlier letters, even in Romans, Paul confronts immediate problems and conflicts, and resolves them by setting them in a wider context of divine purpose as shown above all in the history of the chosen People, drawing often upon the ideas of Jewish apocalyptic literature. In the later letters, a single all-embracing viewpoint is deliberately chosen: it is the viewpoint of the transcendent unity of God's plan, his *mysterion*, for the entire cosmos, including the angelic principalities and powers, and finding its summary fulfilment and embodiment in the risen Christ and his fullness, the Church. It is the 'sapiential' viewpoint, inspired by wisdom traditions of many kinds, and diversely developed in Hebrews and St John's Gospel in the late writings of the New Testament.

The style of the opening chapters of Ephesians must be recognized as indivisibly part of the total communication it is trying to make. This style is solemn, elevated, ceremonious and yet stirring; in a word it is a *liturgical* style, reminiscent of a hymn of praise, thanksgiving and blessing, like the modern 'preface' to our eucharistic prayers; and in fact both have the same source in the traditions of Jewish worship. Thus after the greeting Ephesians begins with 'Blessed be God . . .' and recounts the works for which we bless and praise and give thanks to him. And first and above all we bless God because he has blessed us with every spiritual blessing summed up in Christ, even in the transcendent realm of the heavens. Christ is the focus of God's primal and transcendent will and purpose, through whom we render praise for the *grace* with which he has 'graced' us (the noun and the verb are etymologically connected in the Greek) in his only beloved Son. Through Christ and the blood of his sacrifice we have been redeemed and our sins have been forgiven according to the riches of God's *grace,* which now overflows in us in our experience of insight and understanding of God's mysterious purpose.

The style of this introduction is an expression of rejoicing precisely in the insight bestowed, the style allows us to celebrate in a single enraptured vision the gift and the Giver, the source of a more than cosmic order, pervaded by the active energies of God (cf. verses 19-23): the universe is caught up liturgically into a hymn of praise. And since the praise of God's glory is itself the manifestation of a single predestining purpose from all eternity, so too is the generosity of grace which sets this praise in motion in and through Jesus Christ. Clearly 'grace' here is still a 'realm' or 'regime', but now it is a regime which gives a quality and a character to a kind of cosmic spring and summer, flowering and harvest in Christ. 'Grace' becomes the quality of the apocalypse of the plenitude of the eternal God in the temporal dispensation of creation, redemption and recapitulating fulfilment. All is gift in Christ, except sin; but sin too is swallowed up in forgiveness. Grace is the transcendent heart of the universe. When we are told in 2.8 that we have been saved by grace through faith, not of ourselves or by our works, the particularity of the terms comes as rather a shock; for in the verses immediately preceding grace has once again been hymned in the terms of a transcendent, heavenly order, against a background of 'aeons' – ages or powers, or ages as powers.

In this new context, then, grace may be particularized in the concrete history of conversion, but it embraces this concrete history in Christ and through Christ in an all-inclusive order. All creation is ordered to a gift which unutterably transcends it: the grace of God in Jesus Christ. In consequence everything which comes from Christ and points to Christ can be called 'grace'. This consequence is not in fact explicitly drawn in the New Testament, where the *language* of grace remains in general tied to the purpose of God revealed in Christ and active in conversion to God in Christ. Even in the texts from Ephesians just examined, it is probable that too much has been made of the writer's use of the word *charis*; that is to say, we have probably allowed our interest in *charis* to shift the true centre of the writer's own interest in the passage. Nevertheless, in view of the extended conception of grace in these later Pauline letters, in view too of later conceptions of grace in Christian tradition, it may be legitimate to review in a general way the rest of the New Testament in order to see what other conceptions we may find there which can be assimilated to this wider notion of grace.

One very obvious candidate, it seems to me, is the notion of the 'kingdom of God'. Apart from a few not very significant uses in Luke, the word *charis* does not occur in the Synoptic Gospels; on the other hand, the 'kingdom' or, better, 'reign' (*basileia*) of God is central to the preaching of Jesus. It is in Jesus himself that God's final reign has become present. While the concepts of *charis* and *basileia* are clearly not identical, there does seem to be a considerable overlap (this is even more true of *basileia* and *dikaiosune*, the 'justice' or 'righteousness' of God); and for any modern theology of grace, where the word 'grace' now stands for the whole of God's dealings with man in accordance with his ultimate purpose for him, we may see in the coming of the historical Jesus as the anticipation of God's reign among men, a valuable particularization of the mode in which God's grace becomes active in

27

history. We may read God's gracious purpose on the face and in the words and deeds of the historical Jesus. 'In that same hour he rejoiced in the Holy Spirit and said, "I thank thee, Father, Lord of heaven and earth, that thou hast hidden these things from the wise and understanding and revealed them to babes; yea, Father, for such was thy gracious will" ' (Luke 10.21; the RSV has translated *eudokia*, 'good pleasure', by 'gracious will'. Cf. Mt 11.25).

This very 'Johannine' hymn of praise in Matthew and Luke, especially Johannine in its concluding celebration of the intimate relationship between Father and Son, leads us to ask where we might look in the Johannine writings if we wish to fill out our extended concept of grace. The word *charis* does indeed occur in St John's Gospel four times, all of them in two statements in the Prologue (1.14, 16, 17). On the basis of this restricted use, we could hardly claim that John has a 'theology of *charis*'; but we cannot omit the Johannine writings if we wish to put forward a 'theology of grace'. From this point of view we must simply say that the whole of the Gospel and letters of John are concerned with grace, and that all his characteristic themes are instances of grace. Thus light, life and truth are God's gift to man in Jesus and the Spirit. We may take our cue from the key theme of the *Word* in the prologue, and say that, particularly in the Gospel, John is concerned with God's *communication* of himself to man. This communication is a freely bestowed share not only in the knowledge of God but also of his life. 'Whoever drinks of the water I shall give him shall never thirst, but the water which I shall give him will become in him a spring of water bubbling up to eternal life' (4.14).

According to the prologue, 'grace and truth' (or 'enduring love') '*came to be* through Jesus Christ'. Perhaps part of the force of this verb may be brought out by translating 'happened', 'became event'. This translation has at least the merit of bringing out the sense of movement internal to God's communication of himself. When in the first half of his Gospel, John shows Jesus as the realization of the meaning of the cycle of Jewish festivals, Jesus can be seen as himself an event of enacted liturgy, God's communicated life in motion. In virtue of this communicated life, men become capable of a new life as children of God, drawn up into the union of Father and Son, in their eternal glory. Because we experience in ourselves the welling up of God's communicated life, we have some sense of God's own life as a process of eternal communication, what later theology has spoken of as the processions in the Trinity. Grace, we may say, is the gift of communion with God in Jesus and his Spirit; grace is God's gift of himself; grace is God as gift.

These remarks on grace in the New Testament obviously cannot claim to be regarded as an exhaustive and systematic survey. What we have tried to show is that the language of grace (*charis*) in the Pauline writings undergoes a kind of extension which allows us to review the whole of the revelation of God in Jesus Christ from the vantage point of grace. Grace becomes then an open concept capable of embracing the whole of God's gift of himself to man, and so capable of indefinitely various further particularization. It is not as though we were to itemize God's gifts and call one of them 'grace'; it is rather that 'grace' qualifies the whole of God's self-communication as a gift beyond all telling. We might call 'grace' a *second-level* concept, one which indicates a wholly new dimension of relationship between God and his creation, a transposition of the relationship between Creator and creature into a new mode. We shall return to this suggestion for a theology of grace after looking at some of the ways in which grace has been used as a theological concept in Christian tradition.

CHAPTER TWO

THE TRADITION OF GRACE

It is clearly impossible in a small book like this to try to trace the whole long and complex history of the theology of grace. On the other hand, something, however inadequate, must be said about the dominant figure in the theology of grace, St Augustine of Hippo. By way of postscript to a brief description of his views, we shall outline the later developments of what in the West has been primarily an Augustinian theology of grace, and compare this with the very different tradition of the Greek-speaking East.

It is convenient to review Augustine's teaching on grace in two stages, corresponding in part to the historical sequence of his life. We shall begin with an account of his general views apart from his controversy with Pelagius and his successors, and then see how his theology became more sharply defined in the course of this controversy. We should note, however, that Augustine continued to expound a broader theology of grace even while he was engaged in the Pelagian controversy, for instance in the beautiful series of sermons on the Gospel and the First Epistle of St John. Part of the problem here is again linguistic: it is undoubtedly true that if we look for Augustine's theology of grace in his use of the word *gratia*, it is to the anti-Pelagian treatises we must go; on the other hand, it would be seriously misleading to confine Augustine's understanding of grace to these polemic treatises. It is unfortunate that just because of the pressures of controversy, the official teaching of the Church on grace has found expression in definitions which exclude Pelagianism and, later, 'semi-Pelagianism' (still later, 'Lutheranism', 'Baianism' and 'Jansenism'), since all these controversies have tended to concentrate on limited aspects of God's gracious self-communication. The accumulated weight of these definitions has tended to make the theology of grace, quite inappropriately, into a singularly cumbersome and even repellent affair.

1. St Augustine: the Grace of the New Testament

About the year 412 a catechumen named Honoratus wrote to Augustine from Carthage asking him to expound five passages taken from the Scriptures. Augustine replies that he will find it easier to deal with these questions in a single continuous discourse, and proposes to add a sixth question, 'What is the grace of the New Testament?' This was the origin of the long epistle 140, also known as the book *On the Grace of the New Testament* (PL 33, 538-77). This work is of particular interest to us for two reasons: firstly, as Augustine himself explains, it was written while he was still 'heavily engaged' in the Donatist controversy and just beginning to be involved in the Pelagian one; and secondly, because it provides a conspectus in brief of his views on grace, otherwise scattered through the mass of his varied writings, most of which are occasional, in the sense that they were provoked by the day-to-day occasions of his pastoral office as bishop, either as preacher or as defender of the Church's teaching against the attacks of heretics.

Augustine begins his letter with an exposition of the *order* to be found in human affairs and in creation. As soon as it is born the infant finds itself involved in a life of bodily pains and pleasures, fleeing pain, seeking pleasure: 'to begin life like this is a matter of necessity, to persist in it a matter of will'. But with advancing years and the first glimmerings of reason, it becomes possible for the child to choose a different life, his will assisted by God: the joy of this new life is in the mind, its felicity is interior and eternal. Augustine describes the right use which can be made of created things, pleasure in which can be ordered to the service of the Creator. The rational soul acts well when it preserves the *order* of goodness in created things. To neglect what is above for the sake of what is below is to deteriorate; the aim is by an ordered love, *ordinata caritate*, to turn both oneself and one's body to what is better.

But this Order, with all its neo-Platonist resonances, is not merely 'vertical' but develops in time (a view which Augustine develops interestingly in his treatise *On Music*). The order of the two Testaments, Old and New, exhibits as a succession the order of temporal to eternal felicity:

> God, therefore, wishing to show that even earthly and passing felicity was his gift and should not be hoped for except from him, decided that for the early history of the world there should be put into effect the Old Testament, which belongs to that Old Man from which this life must begin. But it is by the favour (*beneficium*) of God that such occasions of felicity are declared to have been granted, although they belong to this passing life. For while those earthly benefits were openly promised and bestowed, secretly the New Testament was foretold in figure by these events, and grasped by the understanding of a few whom the same grace (*eadem gratia*) had made worthy of the gift of prophecy (col. 539-40).

The 'same grace' in the last phrase is parallel to the 'favour of God' at the beginning of the sentence: there is a single gracious purpose which disposes in order both earthly and eternal felicity, in the individual and in the history of mankind, illuminating the minds of a few even under the Old Dispensation ('Testament' for Augustine refers to a period of history, an epoch, rather than a book) so that they might prophetically foresee the realities of the New Dispensation through the figures of the Old. It is, then, within this context of an abiding and eternal gracious purpose that the grace of the New Dispensation is to be discussed: 'When the fullness of time came, for the grace hidden in the Old Testament to be revealed in the New, God sent his Son' (col. 540, quoting Gal 4.4).

Augustine goes on to discuss the nature of this Son, and to show why there was need for a forerunner, John the Baptist. John was not the light, that is, that Light which illuminates without participating in any other light, and by participating in which all other lights illuminate. This is the first statement in the letter of the theme of participation in the divine nature which is taken up and developed in the next two chapters; and it is important to emphasize it in view of the exaggerated opposition sometimes set up between Augustine and the Greek Fathers on this point.

So for Augustine the grace of the New Testament is that the soul should know its God and be reborn to him by his grace:

> This (spiritual birth) is also called adoption. For we were something before becoming sons of God, and we have received the benefit of becoming what we were not; just as someone who is adopted is not the son of the person who adopts him before he is adopted, although he has to exist in order to be adopted. By this generation of grace that Son is distinguished from us, who although he was the Son of God, came that he might become the son of man, and bestow on us, sons of men, the gift of becoming sons of God . . . He came down, then, that we might rise up; and remaining in his own nature was made a sharer in our nature, so that we, while remaining in our nature, should be made sharers in his nature (col. 541-2).

It is easy to accumulate texts to show Augustine's vivid sense of the reality of this sharing in the divine nature. In a sermon on Psalm 49, he speaks of 'deification' by grace (PL 36,565), and in another sermon (PL 38,909) he says that as new men by the grace of God we should speak the truth 'so that even this mortal flesh which we still have from Adam may itself deserve renewal and transformation in the day of resurrection, and so the whole man deified will cleave to the enduring and unchangeable truth'. We should note that by 'grace' in these passages Augustine regularly means God's loving self-bestowal, a loving-kindness, *misericordia*, in the heart and source of things. This grace effects a real change in those who receive it: spiritual rebirth, justification, adoption, deification, participation in the divine nature; but the effect itself is not usually called 'grace'. Augustine sums up his theology of deification in the letter we have been following in the striking phrase *huius vicissitudinis sacramentum*, the sacrament or mystery of the exchange of natures:

> Make the exchange; become spirit and dwell in him who became flesh and dwelt amongst you. No longer need men despair of becoming sons of God by participation in the Word, when by participation in flesh the Son of God became son of man (col. 542).

The letter now goes on to a consideration of the meaning of the Passion of Christ, which Augustine discusses by expounding Psalm 21 (22). The Passion is seen primarily in the context of the Order of earthly and eternal felicities proper to the two Dispensations; and its meaning is that it reveals this Order in revealing the superiority of the grace of the New Dispensation: in accepting pain and death on the Cross, Christ manifests the superiority of grace by suffering for it. While the moral or exemplary character of this exposition of the meaning of the Passion is evident, it is throughout sustained by a vision of the

34

unity of Christ and the Church which is one of the most insistent themes in Augustine's theology. One short text, taken from his sermons on John (ch. 17; PL 35, 1916) will have to suffice:

> Since the mediator of God and men, the man Christ Jesus, has become head of the Church, they are his members; so he says, 'And I sanctify myself for them.' For what can this mean if not 'I sanctify myself, since they are I myself (*cum et ipsi sunt ego*)?' For those of whom he is speaking are his members, and Christ is one, head and body.

So when Augustine expounds the meaning of the Passion, he envisages it as an abandonment of the bodily life in order to suspend the whole inner being of the New Man, head and members, upon the grace of God: the passage from Old to New is the acting out of a conversion, which in the last resort is to be defined as a replacement of concupiscence by charity, that charity which is a gift of the Holy Spirit. This, Augustine says, is the grace of the New Testament: a suspension of the inner being on the grace of God, and a delight in the ambience of this grace. The consequence of the conversion achieved in head and members by the Passion is that the divine love of charity is bestowed on us in the outpouring of the Spirit: a new being which is a new *love*. The grace of the New Dispensation is an energy of love which rejoices in the recognition that this love itself is a gift; and the recognition is a loving response to the Giver as grace abounding:

> This joy is within, where the sound of praise is sung and heard; so is he praised who is to be loved freely (*gratis*) with all one's heart and soul and mind, and who enkindles a lover for himself by the grace of his Holy Spirit (col. 557).

We see then that what at first sight presented itself as a *moralism* of the Passion is in truth a *spiritualism*:

that is to say, a spiritual identity of Head and members continually supported and vivified by the active presence of the Holy Spirit: a life of the human spirit whose very spontaneity and self-giving are the gift of the Spirit of God and response to that gift. This *is* the grace of the New Dispensation: that by the grace of the Holy Spirit we should *love* grace.

It is in fact to the love of charity that Augustine turns in this long letter after considering sacrifice and the Eucharist in relation to grace. St Augustine has just as much right to the title 'Doctor of Charity' as to his usual title 'Doctor of Grace'; in fact it seems that he is the latter above all because he is the former.

In a sermon he uses the example of earthly and even vicious love, which simply pursues bodily beauty, in order to point to the kind of reality love has in the heart. 'An impure and evil-living man loves a pretty woman; the body's beauty moves him indeed, but within, it is the exchange of love (*amoris vicissitudo*) that is sought.' If he is disappointed and his love is not returned, he loses his love. 'But if he knows that the love is returned (*vicissim amatur*), how much more intensely will he be on fire? She sees him, he sees her, no one sees the love; and yet that very thing (love) is loved which is not seen' (Serm. 34; PL 38,211).

Augustine never ceased to love love. 'I did not yet love and I loved to love . . . I sought something to love, loving to love,' he says in the *Confessions* (3, 1). This is a description of his sinful loves; but in the same sermon from which we have just quoted he says again: 'There is no one who does not love; but the question is what to love. So we are not urged not to love, but to choose what to love' (col. 210). For Augustine love was an enrichment of being ('charity is that precious jewel', he says commenting on 1 John 5, PL 35,2016), as exquisitely sensed as the rustle of rubbed silk or the sliding of spring water over stones; something whose vivid reality must be rediscovered and intensified and illuminated in the love of God. 'He loves thee less who loves something together with thee, which he does not love because of thee. O Love, who art always burning and art never extinguished, Charity, my God, set me on fire! ' (*Confessions*, 10,29). Love is the secret life of the soul called into being in the exchange of love.

> Let no one say, I know not what to love. Let him love his brother, and he will love that very love. For he knows the love with which he loves better than the brother whom he loves. Do you see how God can be better known than your brother? Better known because more present, better known because more inward, better known because more certain. Embrace the love which is God, and embrace God in love. That is the love which joins in fellowship with a bond of holiness all the good angels and all the servants of God, and unites us and them mutually among ourselves in subjection to itself (*De Trinitate,* 8,8; PL 42,957).

This inner reality, better known to us than the brethren we love in charity, is a 'bond of holiness', *vinculum sanctitatis*; and that because it is God, and because it is the Holy Spirit. 'He who loves his neighbour, must love that very love especially. Now "God is love, and who abides in love, abides in God." And so he must love God especially' (ibid.). 'You do not see God: love, and you have him . . . God offers the sum of himself: he cries out to us, Love me, and you will have me; for you could not even love me unless you had me' (Serm. 34. PL 38,211). 'What does God command thee? Love me. You love gold, you are going to seek gold and perhaps not to find it; whoever seeks me, I am with him. Love me, God says to you: there is no middle-man: love itself makes me present to you' (*In 1 Jn* 5. PL 35,2016).

You have begun to love? God has begun to

dwell in you . . . We know that he dwells in us. And how do we know this? Because John himself tells us: 'For he has given us of his Spirit.' And this very fact, that he has given you of his Spirit, how do you know that? Search your heart; if it is full of charity, you have the Spirit of God. How do we know that that is how to know whether the Spirit of God dwells in you? Ask the Apostle Paul: 'For the charity of God is poured forth in our hearts by the Holy Spirit who has been given to us'. (*In 1 Jn* 8. PL 35,2043).

These texts could be multiplied indefinitely. St Augustine did indeed discover a love of God which declared itself in him as abundantly and as richly as any human love which he had known before his conversion. The mystery of the exchange of divine and human natures, *vicissitudinis sacramentum*, is realized as an exchange of love, *vicissitudo amoris*, a presence of the Beloved in the love which is Himself: 'They live mutually (*vicissim*) in each other, he who contains and he who is contained. You dwell in God, but so as to be contained; God dwells in you, but so as to contain you, preventing you from falling' (*In 1 Jn* 8; PL 35,2044). The enrichment of the lover's being is a participation in God's creative love; it is God loving himself in the creature: 'In order then to love God, let God dwell in you, and let him love himself through you' (Serm. 128; PL 38,715).

With the help of the Epistle *On the Grace of the New Testament* we have seen some of the topics which Augustine saw to be relevant to grace, though we have still to deal with the special problem of the insertion of the human will into the divine will for our sanctification. It is clear that for Augustine, charity, the gift of the Holy Spirit, is the core of the grace of the New Dispensation. It is in the quickening of the personal life of love in charity, the exchange of gift for Gift, the opening to the sun of the Spirit, that he discovers the essentially Christian transformation of the soul: a conversion of love.

Towards the end of the Epistle, Augustine turns to the Cross as a symbol of the mystery of charity (PL 33,566). The breadth of charity (he is commenting on Eph 3.14-19) is the cross-piece, referring to good works, for on it the Lord's hands were extended. The length of charity is figured in the upright, and points to long-suffering. The height of charity is shown in the upper part of the upright; here lay the head of the Crucified, which is our hope. But the depth of charity is not seen at all: it is the fixed root of the Cross, whence the whole comes forth; and it signifies the profound mystery of gratuitous grace, *profunditatem gratuitae gratiae*. This is not merely a rhetorical extravagance; it is this mystery of grace, the sacrament or mystery of God's will, which is the theme of the writings against the Pelagians and their successors. It is a mystery of divine charity:

> The love with which God loves us is incomprehensible and unchanging. For he did not begin to love us from the moment when we were reconciled to him by the blood of his Son; but he loved us before the constitution of the world, so that we too should be his sons together with the Only-begotten, before we were at all (*In Jn.*110; PL 35, 1923).

2. St Augustine: the Mystery of God's Will

No attempt will be made in this section to present an account of either the historical course of Augustine's controversy with Pelagius, a British ascetic, sometimes called a monk, who lived in Rome as a spiritual director, or of the detail of the arguments, often confusing; these may be studied in numerous books, some listed in the suggestions for further reading. We shall try instead to bring out what seems to be the central intuition which Augustine was concerned to defend.

It is surely significant that the origin of the controversy may be found in an occasion when a passage from Augustine's *Confessions* was read to Pelagius, who was almost uncontrollably angered by it. The passage contained the famous text from Book 10, 'Grant what you command, and command what you will,' in which Augustine expresses his entire dependence on God's gracious will. It may in fact be argued that the *Confessions* contains the fullest and most attractive expression of Augustine's views on grace and human destiny under God, although, notwithstanding some of the English translations, the word *gratia* occurs rarely in the book; this was at any rate Augustine's own view. And what is perhaps the turning-point of the *Confessions*, at least from our present point of view, is the passage from Book 8 where Augustine describes the moment of his conversion, in the famous scene in the garden after hearing the conversion story told him and Alipius by Pontitianus:

> If I tore at my hair, if I struck myself upon the forehead, if I twined my fingers and clasped my knee, I did these things because I willed to do them. But I might have willed and yet not done them, if the movements of my body had not been obedient to my willing. So many things, therefore, I now did, where the will to act and the power to act were distinct (*ubi non hoc erat velle quod posse*), yet I did not do that which would have contented me incomparably more, and could do as soon as I willed, because I would certainly will as soon as I willed (*et mox, ut vellem, possem, quia mox, ut vellem, utique vellem*). For here the power to do simply is the will to do, and to will the thing was already to do it; and yet the thing was not done. For my body more easily obeyed the

> slightest will of my soul, by moving its limbs
> at its call, than my soul obeyed itself in carry-
> ing out its own strong will, for which noth-
> ing was needed but the will (chapter 8; Tobie
> Mathew translation considerably emended).

Augustine is here analysing with incomparable insight
the paradoxical freedom and servitude of the human
will. On the one hand, the will is manifestly free to
command the other powers of the human being: it
can initiate all sorts of bodily movements 'at will.' On
the other hand, faced by the call to make the choice
of God and truth, it is caught in indecision and con-
tradiction; there is at once a deep will to respond and
consent, and yet a feebleness which prevents this deep
will from realizing itself in an achieved choice which
engages the human being as a whole. Augustine is
verifying for himself the authenticity of St Paul's
analysis of the unredeemed man in Romans 7: 'I do
not understand my own actions. For I do not do what
I want, but I do the very thing I hate . . . I can will
what is right, but I cannot do it,' a text to which
Augustine refers shortly after the passage from the
Confessions just quoted. The issue of Augustine's
struggle is that he hears Continence, chaste mother of
joys begotten by the Lord, encouraging him to cast
himself upon the Lord: 'Why do you stand in yourself
without being able to stand? Cast yourself upon him.'
And when he does so, all the darkness of his doubts is
expelled by the light which is poured into his heart.

The *Confessions* were written between 397–401, before the debate on human freedom and divine grace
with Pelagius; and Augustine's analysis aims at showing the erroneousness of the Manichaean interpretation of this situation of human indecision and enslave-
ment (an interpretation he himself had once shared),
according to which there are two wills, one good and
one evil, in every man, according to his two natures.
But in the light of the controversies with Pelagius,
Augustine's analysis takes on a new significance. What

41

is crucial now is the recognition of two orders or dimensions of human freedom: one which may be called natural, inseparable from any man, where he may choose what it is within his power to do as an independent agent; and another, the order or dimension of grace, where human freedom has itself to be liberated in a choice of God and of itself at once. This second order of human freedom transcends the power of natural human choice; it is a freedom which is elicited by the grace of God, and transfers the whole human being into a new order of human communion with the God of grace. In the one case we have a freedom to act within a region which is subordinate to the human will; in the other, we are given a freedom in a region where the will itself is subordinate to God's higher purpose, where surrender to God in faith is elevation into a new realm.

This somewhat abstract statement of Augustine's central insight must be tested against his own characteristic expression of it, above all in terms of love, *caritas*. Commenting on the text of St John, 'No one can come to me unless the Father who sent me draws him' (6.44), Augustine exclaims that no one can understand his meaning except the lover:

> Show me a lover, and he feels what I am saying. Show me someone who desires, who is hungry, who wanders thirsting in this desert, sighing for the fountain of his eternal homeland; show me one such, and he understands what I am trying to say (*In Jn.* 26; PL 35,1608).

For this drawing is a drawing of love. It is like the 'attraction' which sweets have for children: a drawing by the cord of the heart. As Vergil puts it, quoted by Augustine, 'Each man is drawn by his own pleasure, *voluptas*' (*Eclog.*2,65); it is a drawing by delight, *delectatio*. Conversion for Augustine is conversion by delight into the freedom and new life and vision of the lover. The will to will which is powerless without grace is transformed by delight into an efficacious love, transformed *intrinsically*: delight is the intrinsic character of the blessed life and the life which by the gift of the Holy Spirit is on the way to blessedness. Augustine found support for this interpretation in the passage from Romans quoted above, where Paul goes on to say, 'I delight, *condelector*, in the law of God, in my inmost self.'

In a famous phrase, Augustine speaks of love as a weight: *pondus meum amor meus*. This phrase from the *Confessions* is often enough quoted; but its context is not as well known as it should be. Throughout Book 13 of the *Confessions* Augustine is offering a deeply meditative and highly interiorized interpretation of the first chapter of Genesis, and he comes to deal with the moving of the Spirit over the waters. This Spirit is the Holy Spirit, the more excellent way of charity, the Love of Christ transcending all knowledge; and it is an uplifting opposed to the heavy weight of sinful desires dragging down to the abyss. Augustine asks why it is said of the Spirit alone, and not of the Father and the Son too, that he is as it were in a place, above the waters; and his answer is in terms of an interior physics. It is because the Gift of the Holy Spirit is our rest that he is our proper place: Love raises us up to it as fire flies upward:

> Things which are out of their place are restless; put them in order again, and they are quieted. My weight is my love, and whithersoever I am carried, it is by that I am carried. By thy gifts we are set on fire and carried upwards, we burn within and we go forward . . . With that fire, that good fire of thine, we glow within, and we go, we go upward to the peace of Jerusalem . . . There shall thy goodwill embrace us, so that we desire no more but to remain there for ever (*Conf*.13,9).

Is the 'carrying' of which Augustine speaks here a 'push' or a 'pull'? The question is asked only to focus the proper 'spiritualism' of his mind and his faith. No alternatives so baldly opposed as push or pull are enough to define this spiritualism: the intrinsic spontaneity of his mind's flight to God is the blossoming of a delight which becomes native to it by the gift of the Spirit. The Spirit bears him because the Spirit transforms his mind into its own fire, excites, elicits, and releases its own energy there. Delight is not an exterior object of attraction; it is the supreme spontaneity of the liberated will itself. Like love, delight too is the soul's inner weight: 'Delight is the soul's weight, and orders the soul,' Augustine says in the *de Musica* (6,11; PL 32,1179). The 'drawing' of grace is interior; the efficaciousness communicated to the will is the generation of love itself; to cast oneself on God is to be carried by him.

Against this background we may easily understand why Augustine rejected Pelagius' doctrines so tirelessly. For Pelagius, man is created with free choice, restored to him if need be by baptism, which removes the hindrances due to personal sins. Beyond that he needs only the teaching of Christ for his guide, and his own resolute determination to fulfil it. One rather long text from Augustine will have to serve as a summary of his reasons for rejecting Pelagius' views:

> We say that the human will is divinely helped to accomplish justice in such a way that, besides the fact that man is created with free choice of the will and besides the doctrine by which he is instructed how to live, he receives the Holy Spirit, through whom there comes to be in his mind the delight in and the love of (*delectatio dilectioque*) that supreme and unchangeable good which is God, even now while we still walk in faith and not yet by open vision: so that by this kind of freely bestowed betrothal gift he might be kindled to cleave to the Creator, and be set on fire to attain to participation in that true light, and

44

so might have well-being from him from whom he has being at all. For neither is free choice capable of anything but sin, if the way of truth is hidden; nor, even when what must be done and whither we must strive begins to appear, is anything done or received nor is the good life lived, unless it is also delighted in and loved. Now in order that it might be loved, the charity of God is poured forth in our hearts, not through the free choice which rises from ourselves, but through the Holy Spirit who has been given to us (*De Spiritu et Littera* 3; PL 44,203).

'Love and do what you will' (*In 1 Jn.* 7. PL 35,2033): that is the supreme summary of Augustine's teaching on the life of grace; for that love which is the supreme efficaciousness of the Holy Spirit in our hearts transforms our wills into the act of a sovereign liberty.

In the light of what has been said, it is not surprising that Augustine went on to generalize this teaching on the originality of grace to comprehend the whole of the Christian life. Writing in 396 he says:

In this mortal life, what alone remains to the free will is not that man should accomplish justice, but should turn with begging devotion to him by whose gift man can accomplish justice (*De div.quaest.ad Simplic.* 1,14; PL 40,108).

But he will soon be more precise; the very turning as well as the fulfilment is God's gift: 'So God helps those who turn to him, and abandons those who turn away from him. But even in order that we should turn to him he has to help us' (*De Pecc.Mer.et Rem.* 2,5; PL 44,154). So too the completion of the Christian life is grace:

If our good life is nothing but the grace of God, quite certainly eternal life too, the reward of the good life, is God's grace (*De grat.et lib.arb.*8; PL 44,893).

As the controversy moves into a new phase with the growth of what is now called semi-Pelagianism in the monasteries of southern Gaul, Augustine develops this teaching in relation to the questions of the first movement of faith (*initium fidei*) and final perserverance. We shall simply note here the relation between predestination and grace for Augustine: 'The only difference between grace and predestination is that predestination is preparation for and of grace, grace the actual bestowal' (*De Praed. Sanct.* 10; PL 44,974).

> It is we, then, who will, but God works in us the willing too; we who work, but God works in us the working too, according to his good will . . . For since our heart is not in our power, but is sustained by the divine help to ascend and taste what is above . . . to whom are we to give thanks if not to our Lord God who is doing this, who by liberating us from the abyss of this world by such a favour, has chosen us and predestined us before the foundation of the world? (*De Dono Persev.* 13; PL 45,1013. Note the key-texts from Phil 2.12-13 and Eph 1.4).

'Our heart is not in our power'. For Augustine, the heart is the organ of human and divine love, and its depths are unfathomable. Commenting on the text of Psalm 41 (42), 'Deep calls to deep', *Abyssus abyssum invocat*, he sees man's heart as an abyss, yet one which lies bare and open to God's eyes (PL 36,473). The mystery of the human heart responds to the mystery of God's will, the *sacramentum voluntatis Dei*, according to the Vulgate translation of Eph 1.9, what a medieval Augustinian, William of St Thierry, called the 'sacrament of all sacraments'. Pursuing this play on the senses of the Latin *sacramentum*, we may speak of a sacramental union of divine and human wills as the fine point of Augustine's theology of grace: *unitas spiritus*, the reality of all the liturgical sacraments, uniquely fulfilled in the incarnate manifestation of the Sacrament of God's love, Jesus Christ, the exemplar of our grace.

3. The Greek Tradition

St Augustine's writings were going to provide the context for all subsequent discussion of grace in the Latin West. The Church in the East, however, was largely untouched by what were seen as purely Western controversies, although Pelagianism was glanced at in a joint condemnation of Nestorius and Caelestius, one of Pelagius' followers, at the Council of Ephesus in 431. If we examine the Greek tradition with the theology of grace in mind, we discover on the one hand an abundant use of the language of *charis*; on the other, we meet certain themes which modern interpreters, at least, have frequently associated with the theology of grace.

The difficulty here is not unlike that which we have already had to face in reviewing the New Testament evidence. There was no Greek Augustine; and there exists no single treatise in Greek which has *charis* for its explicit theme, for instance, by having *charis* in its title. The linguistic evidence is systematically surveyed in Lampe's *Patristic Greek Lexicon*, which needs several columns to cover the ground. According to the Lexicon, *charis* is used in general of God (Father, Son and Holy Ghost) as source of grace; it is used to speak of sanctifying grace (a Latin category!), its necessity for Christian life, and in relation to human cooperation, especially in the practice of self-denial and virtue; it is used to speak of certain effects of grace – purification, sonship etc. – and in the mystical life; grace and sin are connected, as are also grace and nature; grace is contrasted with works, there is talk of Adam's grace before the Fall, and the language of grace is also used to speak of ecclesiastical office, prophecy, miracles, the Scriptures. Finally *charis* is used in various Christological contexts and in some other scattered references, for instance, to speak of the beauty of the face of the martyr.

We may wonder how seriously we should take this classification, however useful any considered classification might be of material of such extent and diversity. What seems to be clear is that there is no single dominant perspective, such as emerged from our brief examination of St Augustine. This is not necessarily a disadvantage; it is valuable to be reminded that Christian theology can be conscious of grace without having to treat it thematically. We must however note that modern interpreters of the Eastern tradition, especially writers in the Russian Orthodox tradition living in the West, have claimed to see an alternative to the Western theology of *grace* in an Eastern tradition of *deification* (*theosis*), indeed to see this alternative as a critique of Western theology. This claim has been taken seriously by many modern Roman Catholic theologians, so much so that it has become almost a theological commonplace to contrast the Western theology of grace and the Eastern theology of deification. Without being able properly to substantiate my own view, I believe that it would be preferable to see these theologies as overlapping rather than in competition, so that a theology of grace might have much to learn from a theology of deification, and yet retain a distinct perspective in which certain elements essential to Christian revelation come into sight in a way which is not possible within the perspective proper to the Eastern tradition.

We may take as a definition of deification the statement made by the late fifth-century writer known as Pseudo-Dionysius: 'Deification is assimilation to and union with God so far as he is accessible' (*Ecclesiastical Hierarchy* 1,3; PG 3,376). When the theology of deification is seen as an alternative to the theology of grace, both deification and grace are seen as alternative ways of describing union with God; yet, as we have seen in our review of the New Testament, union with God is by no means the primary sense of the word *charis*. The primary sense is that of free giving, the mystery of God's incomprehensible generosity, something which is brought out incomparably in St Augustine's awareness of his total experience as sustained by and responsive to the God who gives himself. From the New Testament and St Augustine we may gradually learn to appreciate the texture of our entire experience as a disclosure of God's free generosity in our free response to that generosity.

The connexion between *theosis* and *charis*, deification and grace, is not in fact often made in the Greek tradition in any systematic way. St Maximus the Confessor (seventh century) provides a good example of a more systematic use:

> No created thing is capable by nature of producing deification, since it is not capable of grasping God either; it belongs to divine grace alone to bestow deification in due proportion on existing things (*Quaestiones ad Thalassium* 22; PG 90,321).

What is in any case certain is that the Greek theology of deification belongs to the 'cosmic' perspective which is characteristic of Greek theology in general. How we should evaluate this perspective is a much more delicate matter. There are some who would see in this perspective a distortion of the Gospel by Hellenistic 'physics', and there is no doubt that theologies of grace even in the West have sometimes seemed to reify grace, to make it into a 'thing', under the influence of philosophical categories taken from Greek tradition, both Christian and pre-Christian. On the other hand there is no doubt that the cosmic perspective of deification allows us to appreciate the reality of our transformation in Christ. Further, it must not be too readily assumed that the 'physical' language of Greek theological tradition should be read 'literally'; the language is commonly poetic or at least heightened in

49

such a way that it is meant to communicate by metaphor the uniqueness of the real processes in which we are involved by becoming one man and one body in Christ. Consider, for instance, this fine text from St Cyril of Alexandria, commenting on words from the Gospel of St John:

> He is raised up and anointed and sanctified for our sakes, so that through him grace should spread to all, being given already to nature in him and preserved for the whole race of man. And so he says, 'I am the Way', a way as it were through which divine grace has descended to us, raising up and sanctifying and glorifying and deifying nature in Christ as first and origin (*Thesaurus* 20; PG 75,333).

Here again grace and deification are connected; what is unmistakably 'Greek' is the condensation of salvation in the incarnate humanity of Christ as the origin of a renewed human 'nature'. The historical life of Jesus, from nativity to resurrection, is condensed into a deified human nature of Christ, the originating source of our deification. We may compare St Gregory of Nyssa on the Eucharist:

> The reason why God, when he revealed himself, united himself with our mortal nature was to 'con-deify' humanity by its participation in the divinity. In consequence, by means of his flesh, which is constituted by bread and wine, he implants himself in all believers, following out the plan (economy) of grace. He fuses himself with their bodies so that mankind too, by its union with what is immortal, may share in incorruptibility (*Oratio catechetica*,37. Translation of Library of Christian Classics, vol.III, modified, following revised Greek text; PG 45,97).

These two texts from Cyril and Gregory are clear examples of a 'realism' of redemption, which associates all humanity with what Gregory calls Christ's 'God-bearing flesh', the humanity of Christ deified in the Incarnation. When the language of grace appears in contexts like this, it too tends to share in this realism of an incarnational economy.

The final step in the development of Eastern Orthodox theology was taken in the writings of St Gregory Palamas (fourteenth century), who holds a position in the East not unlike that which has been held by St Thomas Aquinas in the Catholic West. To attempt even a brief sketch of his views would be impossible here; all we may do is to hint at the central experience which seems to animate his theology. This seems to be the contemplative experience of entering into the glory of God, as for instance the Apostles did at the Transfiguration of Jesus on Mount Tabor. This radiance of divine glory is regarded as an 'uncreated energy' of God, distinct from the divine essence yet not part of creation. 'Uncreated grace', then, is for Palamas the divine life itself, as bestowed on man: the manifest radiance of the divinity rather than the inaccessible darkness of the divine essence. By participating in this radiance man is transformed, deified; above all, for Palamas, taken up into the source of deification. The primary sense of grace here is the emanation of uncreated divine life, not its created effects in the man who receives it.

What this last example should make clear is that the Greek tradition of deification has to be understood as ascent as well as descent, within the context of a mystical contemplation as well as the context of transforming gift. The same Gregory of Nyssa who speaks of 'God-bearing flesh' is also the author of numerous ascetical and mystical treatises, and the Pseudo-Dionysius became even in the West a primary source for a mystical tradition, more and more divorced there from a speculative theology of the schools. The central tradition of the Eastern Church has never had to suffer from this divorce of mysticism from speculation; its

51

theology has always been contemplative and liturgical, at least in principle if not always in everyday practice. We may illustrate this contemplative theology of deification with a beautiful text from Gregory of Nyssa, and so bring to an end our brief survey of the Greek contribution to a theology of grace:

> For those who look towards the true God receive within themselves the characteristics of the divine nature; so too, those who turn their minds to the vanity of idols are transformed into the objects which they look at, and become stones instead of men. Turned thus to stone by the worship of idols, human nature became immovable and unable to advance; it had become stiff with the chill of idolatry. And therefore the 'Sun of Justice' rose in this cruel winter, the spring came, the south wind dispelled the chill, and together with the rising of the sun's rays warmed everything that lay in its path. Thus mankind, that had been chilled into stone, might become warm again through the Spirit, and receiving heat from the rays of the Word, might again become as 'water leaping up into eternal life' (commenting on *Song of Songs* 2.10-12, *In Cant.*5; PG 44,866; tr. Musurillo).

4. Aquinas to Luther and Trent

We shall end this highly selective survey of the tradition of grace by looking at some medieval developments in the Latin West.

In this as in most other fields of theology St Thomas Aquinas made an outstanding contribution. In his later writings we may find in a precise, articulated and publicly accessible form a great deal of St Augustine's spiritual insight, together with a considerable understanding of what the Greek tradition has to offer,

essence of the human soul, had some unfortunate consequences for the theology of grace. At least in the case of Eckhart, it is extremely difficult to overcome a sense of uneasiness as to just how God's gracious presence in the soul is to be distinguished from the essence of the soul itself. It may be that this ambiguity arises from the effort to talk about an *experience* of the essence of the soul, and to talk about it in the Neo-Platonist perspective which dominated this speculative mysticism. Although Eckhart has many modern defenders of his orthodoxy, the present writer feels some sympathy for those who have detected a resemblance between Eckhart's mysticism and the speculative mysticism of the Vedanta.

In the context of this book again, this may be the best way to introduce the complex figure of Martin Luther, although the massive bulk of his writings and the huge output of interpretation of them are daunting to any superficial student of his work such as the present writer. One thing at least seems certain: that Luther was a genuine novelty in the Christian tradition. Looking back at him from a distance of four centuries of European history, it is clear that his was a voice of the future, while the rejoinder of the Council of Trent was undoubtedly a voice of the Christian past.

It is of course true that Luther emerged out of late medieval theology, and yet even in his earliest writings, notably the first commentary on the Psalms, his distinctive individuality shows itself clearly. If from one point of view the tradition of speculative mysticism may be seen as the last attempt to integrate scholastic theology and Christian experience, Luther's writings from the first show the signs of a powerful effort to construct a new style of theology which would make sense of a new idiom of human and Christian experience. Looking back at him from our own times, it may perhaps be said very simply that Luther was trying to create a *personal* theology, by discovering in the Bible a *personal* relationship to God in Christ: a theology expressed in terms of 'I', the self, rather than of 'the soul'. And yet it was truly a theology he was trying to formulate, a way of expressing the whole human situation before the God who revealed himself in the Bible, and not just a piece of piety. Inevitably his successors produced a new sort of scholastic orthodoxy and a new sort of pietism; but Luther himself should not be judged in terms of either of these.

Luther's theology of grace, then, has a dramatic style: it expresses the emergence into history of a new kind of self-awareness, and yet as a response within the Christian tradition (Augustine in particular) to God. His violent rejection of scholastic metaphysics – Aristotle, Pseudo-Dionysius – is surely to be understood as an expression of the painful effort to free himself from categories which could not support this new kind of self-awareness and self-understanding. Here grace becomes above all the experience of a God who allows himself to be encountered in a face-to-face relationship by one who deeply experiences himself to be a sinner.

That this new style of theology was and remains ambiguous, that, for instance, it modifies the declaratory force of doctrinal definitions conceived of as objective statements independent of the individual believer, must certainly be admitted. Yet the response of the Council of Trent in its lucid and balanced decree on Justification is in truth no response to Luther's genuine innovations. It may not unfairly be regarded as a strong re-affirmation of the classical tradition of Christian theology in the West, without any real understanding of the deep shift of theological consciousness which had taken place.

At this point we cannot avoid raising a question which has so far been avoided: why is the main document in which the Church's teaching on grace is to be found a decree on *justification*? What is the meaning and significance of this term, which has such an un-familiar sound to the Christian, or at least the Catholic Christian today? To answer this question properly would require another book, at least as long as the present one. Alternatively, the present book might have been written from a quite different perspective, the perspective precisely of justification. Just as in the case of the language of grace, we must begin by recognising that the notion of justification has a history, and that the word has not always had the same meaning.

For many modern exegetes, the doctrine of justification is the centre of St Paul's gospel, and even more, the central doctrine of the New Testament, the doctrine which makes unified sense of the whole of biblical revelation. If this claim is to be made plausible, the notion of justification must be taken very broadly indeed, to refer to that sovereign intervention of God in history whereby he vindicates his own sovereignty and 'justice', exhibiting this sovereign justice in an assembly of those he has made his own by 'justifying' them. God exhibits his own transcendence by restoring the due order of things to his own glory. At the centre of this 'apocalypse' or manifestation of his sovereignty is the cross of Jesus Christ, where sin is revealed as rebellion against the glory of God and overcome in death and resurrection. The new order to God's glory established in the death and resurrection of Jesus Christ is made available to all those who submit themselves in faith to God in Christ. Baptism above all is the efficacious expression of the submission of faith and its acceptance, and the incorporation of the believer into God's order by way of a sharing in the death and resurrection of Christ.

What we may notice, from St Augustine onwards, and especially in high and in late scholasticism, is a progressive narrowing of this broad notion of justification. Justification begins to be conceived of primarily as something which takes place in the individual believer, without explicit reference to Jesus Christ, and without explicit reference to the sacramental economy of God's order. The process of justification in the individual is more and more closely analysed as a privileged instance of the interplay of divine power and human freedom, of God and man in general. From one point of view, the Western theology of grace has been dominantly a theology of *conversion*, marked by the experience of those two great converts, Paul and Augustine. We may say that while the scholastic analysis of this moment of conversion became more and more abstractly general, Luther revived the Western theology of grace as conversion by making the *experience* of conversion the whole and permanent meaning of the theology of grace. *Simul iustus et peccator*, at once just and a sinner, is the apt rendering of this experience of conversion commended as the permanent expression of man's existence before God.

It is now widely recognized that Luther cannot be properly understood except against the background of late scholastic theology, especially the nominalist tradition beginning with William of Ockham. If we try to enter sympathetically into the theological concerns of this period of theology in the fourteenth and fifteenth centuries, we may see it as a resolute attempt to insist on the transcendence of God, perhaps as a counterbalance to a Christendom increasingly involved in power politics and superstition. A distinction on which great stress is laid throughout this period is one between God's absolute power, *potentia absoluta*, and his power within the limits of his own institution, *potentia ordinata*. Thus for Scotus, in the order of things in fact established by God, it is certainly true that a 'habit' (a stable disposition qualifying the individual) of charity is required so that God's good pleasure, *acceptatio divina*, may rest upon the individual. But this 'habit' is finite and created; it is impossible that God's power should be restricted by any finite, created thing; God's absolute power must be such that he could accept by his good pleasure even someone who lacked this habit. The only restriction on God's absolute power is that it cannot be internally self-contradictory. The whole created order is the contingent expression of a divine creative will which could be otherwise; nothing in this created order can constrain the divine will. Hence the famous Scotist theory of the 'motive of the Incarnation' (though in fact this thesis is to be found in the Franciscan school as early as the *Summa* once attributed to Alexander of Hales): the Son of God would have become man even if Adam had not sinned, the Incarnation is not necessarily redemptive.

It has been rightly remarked about this thesis that it amounts to a total vision of the universe. The only adequate object of God's will is his own glory; other objects of his will fall into a descending order of priority. So the Incarnation precedes any sequence of created causes and effects in the historical order, though this too is an expression of the same divine will and is in fact ordered to the glory of God by way of the Incarnation. It is perhaps not surprising that some modern Scotists have hurried to find in Teilhard de Chardin a witness to the prophetic insight of their chosen master.

What seems to stand out more and more clearly in this late scholastic theology is a kind of dissociation of God from human experience. If God's good pleasure is such that it *need* not express itself creatively in a transformation of the creature by charity; and if further, as Scotus held, it is impossible to be aware of charity even if one has it; then one may adore God in his inscrutable will but one can hardly delight in his gift of himself to the creature. But these are enormous topics, open to a variety of interpretations, and the present writer cannot claim to feel at home in late medieval theology. It is certain that the early Luther, anxious like his predecessors to 'let God be God', *velle*

Deum esse Deum, broke his way through to an experience of a transcendent God of mercy, by way of a conversion experience which in his later years he liked to recall, his famous experience in the tower when the meaning of Romans 1.17 first became plain to him. 'Justification by faith alone' is Luther's response to his late medieval tradition, an expression of the place of experience at the heart of Christian life, forgiveness as the purest revelation of divine transcendence.

The reply of Catholic orthodoxy at the Council of Trent was, then, inevitably framed as a theology of justification. Quite exceptional care was taken in its formulation, and a serious attempt made to go beyond the disputes of Scotists and Thomists to the sources of Catholic tradition; both Luther and Trent are heirs of St Augustine. 'Justification' is given a broader sense, explicitly including 'sanctification' and a reference to its various 'causes': the final cause is said to be the glory of God and Christ and eternal life; the efficient cause the merciful God; the meritorious cause Jesus Christ in his Passion; the instrumental cause the sacrament of baptism; and finally the formal cause is said to be that divine justice by which we are made just in ourselves. And yet, in spite of this broadening of perspective, it still seems true to say that the Tridentine account of justification, like Luther's, reflects a special and limited view of biblical revelation: the centre of interest is what happens to man, and indeed the individual man, not what God does in his self-manifestation. It has been one of the merits of the work of Karl Barth (one wonders how he would have liked this formula) in our own times, especially perhaps his early commentary on the Epistle to the Romans, to remind us of a 'theocentric' view of justification, in this prolonging a Calvinist tradition.

The Tridentine decree also insisted on the reality of the change brought about by justification, as opposed to a Lutheran view, trapped by a literalist reading of biblical forensic metaphor, which saw justification as 'imputation'. The Tridentine teaching hardened in later years into a position which seemed to divorce the gift of grace from the Giver; and it is this post-Tridentine controversial view which has been attacked by Protestant theologians, not without reason. But perhaps the deeper question concerns the categories and the procedures by which we attempt to understand the 'real'. It does not seem that the Tridentine decree is seriously aware that a long tradition through which the apprehension of reality had been mediated, was now under serious question; and it is clear enough that the Protestant reformers themselves were not aware of the seriousness of their challenge to conventional presuppositions about the nature and availability of the real. This problem is still with us in an acute form, bearing not only on the theology of grace but on the whole of Christian revelation, on God and man: how and where are we to situate ourselves so as to put our finger on the really real?

From the time of Trent onwards, a distinctively Roman Catholic theology of grace comes into being, consciously bounded against the theologies of the Reformers. Within that Roman Catholic tradition differences and even violent disputes were still possible, but one has a curious sense that the tradition had lost contact with the history of human experience, to their mutual impoverishment. Faced by the bewildering confusion of distinctions, polemics and condemnations (on which Pascal's *Provincial Letters* throw a sharp and lively light at a time of particularly bitter dispute), the average student of theology tended to avoid the theology of grace altogether. Perhaps in our own times it has become possible to make a new approach to the topic.

CHAPTER THREE

A PERSPECTIVE FOR
A THEOLOGY OF GRACE

1. The Primary Sense of Grace

If this hasty and inadequate survey of the history of the theology of grace has been even partially successful, it will have become clear that grace has been understood in many ways in the history of Christianity. If we reflect on this history we may see that the variety of ways in which grace has been understood is not merely a queer feature of the theology of grace. When the language of grace changes in one way or another, when grace becomes associated with one theme rather than another, these changes bring to light deep changes in the fundamental understanding of the relation between God and man. For reflection on grace is a reflection precisely on this relationship. If we wish to maintain that in some absolutely basic sense the relationship between God and man is as it were eternally the same, we must at least allow that the historical event of Jesus Christ is the typical revelation of this relationship, the key to its understanding; and we must also allow that our understanding of the relationship changes in accordance with the change in our understanding of God and man.

Perhaps we should examine more closely what might be meant when we speak on the one hand of an 'eternal' and unchanging relationship between God and man, and on the other, of a changing understanding of this relationship. We want to say that God is utterly transcendent, that he is not subject to the vicissitudes of temporal change either in the cosmos or in history. We want to say that somehow the relationship shares in the absolute and eternal character of God himself. But we must be careful here. For in the first place it is precisely as subject to time that God has created man in the cosmos and in history; and in the second place, 'creation' itself is a notion which has been subject to historical change. It is surely important not to take for granted some single model of creation to which we then merely add a few extrinsic features which take account of the historical coming of Jesus Christ, as though this merely happened *within* a pre-established natural order. We shall discuss this second point in more detail later. For the moment it is the first point which needs to be considered patiently and cautiously and honestly; we have to learn to recognize that our effort to understand the ultimate and absolute truth of God's eternal purpose for man is an effort in time and in history, and shares in the flux of all man's conceptions of himself and of God. We can only use the word 'God' to refer to what is absolutely transcendent; but we can only use it in a finite, relative and historically contingent way. And we can only use the word 'man' to refer to the bearer of an historical process for which he is fitted by endowments which may be definite but which we cannot define except in an 'open' way – perhaps by saying, 'Man is capable of history, of generating the new.' And it follows that precisely because we want to be able to affirm the absolute transcendence of God – God as always greater – we must allow that God is he who surpasses and contains *whatever* new thing man brings forth historically: God always newer. We may even venture to say that the whole point of theology is to exhibit the transcendent novelty of God in relation to the novelty of man.

Reflections of this apparently abstract and world-historical sort may be given some evident concreteness if we relate them to the changes in the understanding of ourselves and of God which each one of us undergoes in the course of our lives. It is surely a plain fact of experience that we change in our understanding of God and of ourselves. The changes do not necessarily exhibit themselves as a continuous growth; there are shifts and abrupt discontinuities, and part of the task of our lives – or, in a sense, the only and ultimate task of our lives – is to discover and lay bare to ourselves the underlying continuity of this change, to exhibit the change as growth without pretending to be able in advance to predetermine the sense of this growth. The sense of this growth, its direction, economy and meaning, is what we apprehend as our destiny, God's mysterious plan for each one of us; we discover, progressively, God and ourselves within this mysterious plan.

We are accustomed to consider those people wise who have learned by experience to undergo and shape by response to it their destiny in God's plan; and if theology aspires to the condition of wisdom, *sapientia,* then it too must be prepared to reflect on the plan of God in the history of the individual and of mankind. The theology of grace must surely always seek to be 'sapiential', to meditate on an experience of God and man and discern as far as possible the meaning implicit in this experience. We believe as Christians that God's plan for man is the eternally preordained union of man with God which is the whole meaning of human destiny; but it will be no use simply to rehearse a theology of grace which tells of a union of God and man in terms which we cannot recognize in our own deepest firsthand experience. Such an account would only be useful as a model for our own attempt to speak in our own voice. On the other hand, the problematic and even dubious character of such an attempt is evident. Who would dare to claim so clear an insight into the awareness of God and man in our time as to be prepared to formulate a theology of grace in terms of this awareness, given the enormous variety of explicit doctrines of God and man competing for our assent today (even the non-Christian ones are hardly to be dismissed out of hand), and, what is more, the confusion of indistinct awareness of God and man below the level of doctrine?

It may be that just this way of formulating the problem is misleading. It may be that we should not attempt first to formulate our doctrines of God and man and then to relate God and man in a theology of the preordained union of these isolated and thus preconceived terms. Rather we should perhaps speak out of an indistinct awareness of the union as it is already made known to us, and allow our discourse to have an openness to the multiple understanding and experience of God and man which we merely *sense* to be ours today. It is at any rate this second alternative which will be adopted here.

For Christians there can be no question but that the centre of our awareness of the union of God and man is Jesus Christ. Consequently the centre of any theology of grace must also be Jesus Christ. But we must remember that just as we avoided an approach to the theology of grace which would consist in the connection of two previously known terms, God and man, so too Jesus Christ is not in the first place to be looked at as the point of connection of these known terms. It is certainly true that we find in Scripture and the tradition of the Church formulations of the union of God and man in Jesus Christ, some of which seem to have a definite and definitive character, and there can be no question of ignoring them. But even in the New Testament there are different ways in which the inspired writers represented Jesus Christ; and the traditional definitions of the Church's Christology already show presuppositions about God and man with which we can learn to sympathize but which we do not necessarily share.

When we take Jesus Christ as the centre of our theology of grace, then, we do so in the sense that in our experience of him in faith we are given privileged access to the mutual and incomprehensible mysteries of God and man in their preordained union. It is in Jesus Christ, given in our experience of faith, that we are to try to understand more deeply the terms 'God', 'man', 'preordained' and 'union', these terms which reverberate in our experience today with associations which could not have occurred to our Christian fore-runners. In Jesus Christ these terms come together as a family, as a web of associations; and it is as a member of this family that we wish to try to locate the term 'grace'.

The experience of Jesus Christ in faith is both simple and complex. It is simple in the sense that it emerges in the utterly elementary gesture in which we can open our hearts to Jesus and touch him with the finger of faith. It is complex in the sense that it has an in-definitely wide range of particular public occasions and embodiments, notably participation in the Euch-arist and reading or hearing the Scriptures, and also, less clearly but at least sometimes no less powerfully, in meetings and sharings with other human beings and even in the world of non-human nature, as in Hopkins's poem, 'The Windhover.' It is important to recognize that this experience of Jesus Christ in faith involves us in going beyond the distinction between 'objective' and 'subjective' ways of talking which has become deeply ingrained in our tacit understanding of ourselves and the world. There are many ways in which philosophers and others have tried to go beyond this distinction, conventionally described as 'Cartesian', even in non-religious and non-theological areas of understanding. To try to go beyond the distinction is not to deny that the distinction can and even must be made, but it is to deny that the distinction is as pri-mary and fundamental as it has sometimes seemed to be. For our purposes here it will be sufficient to try to show that our experience of ourselves and the world is not in fact adequately analysed in terms of a dis-tinction between 'objective' and 'subjective' understanding; and consequently that our experience and understanding of Jesus Christ in faith is still less adequately analysed in such terms. And if this is accepted, then grace too is not *either* 'subjective' *or* 'objective': grace is not *either* 'subjective experience' *or* 'objective fact.'

It should be observed that in the classical theology of the Roman Catholic tradition, especially in the work of St Thomas Aquinas, any distinction into subjective and objective categories was surpassed and grounded in an understanding of *being, esse,* prior to all possible distinctions and capable of an indefinite variety of particular realizations. Thus when St Thomas spoke of grace as a kind of 'spiritual being', *esse spirituale,* he was not in the first place attributing to it *either* an 'objective' *or* a 'subjective' character, though the term 'spiritual' implies an identification of grace with the help of categories which we may not find obvious today. Yet it must be said that we do not easily talk about 'being' today; we do not easily allude to the unity of all that is by speaking of 'being.' It seems likely that in our own times an equivalently acceptable primary theme of understanding – and one which might lead us back to reflection on *being* – would be *meaning.*

It is of great importance in the present context to insist that the term 'meaning' is in constant and common use without any reflective analysis of the meaning of 'meaning'. Of course a variety of attempts has been made to locate and define what might be meant by 'meaning', but more important than any of these theoretical essays is the ordinary, everyday, undefined use of the term. This everyday and indistinct use of the term is what we have to start from if we wish to present something like a theology in terms of meaning as an alternative to a theology in terms of being. 'Meaning' seems to have for us today the same kind of indistinct universality and obviousness which perhaps 'being' had for earlier epochs in the Western tradition

67

(not, say, in the Far East). This obviousness has its deep significance; it would seem to indicate a deep shift in our consciousness of the way things are and the way in which we find ourselves 'in the world'.

This is clearly not the place in which to embark on some general investigation of 'meaning'; indeed it will seem to many readers, perhaps, that this discussion has already strayed too far from its prescribed theme. Yet since it is the ambitious purpose of this small book to suggest a perspective for the theology of grace in our own times, we shall allow ourselves some brief general considerations of 'meaning' so as to provide a point of reference for a theology of grace as meaning. Just as St Thomas, say, ordered the whole indefinite range of *being* by referring to *substances*, independently existing entities, we in our turn need to locate the whole indefinite range of *meaning* by referring to some privileged locus and original instance. The proposed instance here runs as follows: meaning is that praxis, that process and activity, by which the world to which man belongs becomes the world which belongs to man. We may particularize this instance still further by seeing meaning as a kind of game. We transform the world to which we belong by taking it up into the world of the games we play. Meaning, that is to say, is historical; it assumes a world prior to man into a world of human communication, by work, play, dance, travel, love, conversation, reflection – the totality of human life and death, in the continuity of a humanity which inwardly transforms the biological into the historical order. The possibilities of meaning are indefinite, which is not to say that they are infinite, but only that they have no ascertainable bound, each particular realized possibility being of course finite (compare 'being').

Provided that we do not allow ourselves to identify meaning in dominantly 'personalist' terms, it may be useful to consider the way we understand each other in human communication. In fact we understand each other in an enormous variety of ways: simply leaving each other room to pass in the street (this is already a highly sophisticated activity, contrasted in our practice with the alternative of pushing each other into the gutter); transacting business with each other in virtue of roles which we adopt for the purpose; explaining each other to ourselves, to others or to each other, in terms of more or less sophisticated sociological or psychological stereotypes; appreciating each other in terms of historical or literary traditions; a silent communion of love which by way of words, gestures, a shared life, has gone beyond words into a breathing stillness.

Now if Jesus were only a man who lived in Palestine many centuries ago, we would have to try to understand him in many of these ways, though we could only expect to meet him through the reports of those who knew him. But in fact those who tell us about him claim that we may meet him in some other way; that although he lived long ago in the past, he is present personally to those who turn to him in a movement which is called faith, and which he himself makes possible. This new kind of meeting is a new kind of understanding and a new kind of meaning, which extends the whole range of meaning and understanding of each other we had before and modifies it pervasively. Those who turn to Jesus in faith become aware of new possibilities of meeting other people and understanding them. We may think of it as a new dimension of the world of meaning. It is neither (in the first place) 'objective' nor 'subjective', but modifies the whole process of human meaning: it modifies our understanding of meaning itself and of its possible boundaries; it modifies our sense of 'man' and 'God'. It is within this enlarged world of meaning, given in the experience of Jesus Christ in faith, that we wish to locate grace.

At this point I want to make it clear that a definite theological option is going to be made: I am going to introduce the word 'destiny' and place it in the fore-going discussion by calling 'destiny' the sense and the direction of the process of human meaning. Destiny emerges in the process of meaning as the question 'Why?' It is a question which can be asked in many different tones of voice, and it is a question which may be rejected or evaded or suppressed. That people do, however, ask the question cannot be denied, nor that they often ask it as though it were the most important question any human being could ask about himself or about humanity, even when, and perhaps above all when, he asks it in despair: in the grip of the con-viction that the question can have no answer, that human destiny is meaningless, that the process of meaning has no sense or direction, that meaning is internally inconsistent.

Christianity consists in the claim that (1) the why-question has a unique answer, that human destiny is determinate; (2) this destiny is disclosed in the destiny of Jesus Christ; (3) the destiny of Jesus Christ is a predestination, the fulfilment of the purpose of God; (4) this predestined destiny is ours to share in by way of our communion with Jesus Christ in faith.

The clearest summary of this fourfold claim in the New Testament is to be found in the hymn of thanks-giving at the beginning of the Epistle to the Ephesians, which was discussed earlier in this book. Here we draw attention especially to the refrain which punctu-ates the passage: 'to the praise of his glory.' The destiny to which man is summoned, the primordial and the ultimate sense of the process of meaning which transforms nature into history, is an activity of praising in which the why-question is absorbed and overcome. Reduced to the ultimate extremity of de-spair we go beyond in a hymn of praise. When the Jewish editors of the Old Testament called what we now call the Psalter or Book of Psalms *tehillim*, 'praises', they may not have been much concerned about literary genres, but they were aware of the

70

ultimate point of liturgical celebration and the celebration of life: the praise of God's glory, even in the abject desolation of abandonment by God. When Jesus cries out on the Cross (Mt 27.46), 'My God, why have you forsaken me?', he is using the opening words of Ps 22, addressed to the holy one 'enthroned on the praises of Israel' (v.3), and which concludes with a song of praise. The desolation, the ultimate extremity of the why-question, is the way to its overcoming in praise, in resurrection, in glory.

When Jesus 'having loved those of his own who were in the world loved them to the end', utterly and comprehensively (Jn 13.1), he also explained in the so-called 'high-priestly prayer' (Jn 17) the meaning of this love. The disciples of Jesus, consecrated by Jesus' own consecration of himself, are to be united with him in an inward communion and exchange of love which is the multiplication into a more comprehensive unity of the inward communion and exchange of love between Jesus and his Father, in the glory which Jesus shared and shares with the Father before the foundation of the world. The whole of the discourse in chapters 13-17 of St John's Gospel is a reflective disclosure of the final sense of the why-question: how it is to be asked and how answered. And it is a farewell discourse, which reveals the answer through a separation permanently disclosed in the death of Jesus who is the Way, the Truth and the Life: the answer is a way of life through death, the death of Jesus which is the final fulfilment of his destiny, his sending by the Father. Struggle against it as we may, we have to be lifted up with Jesus into the transcendence of his Cross in a common destiny with him. This is the final expression of the love of the Father and the love with which Jesus loved and loves his own: it must be the living and luminous centre of any theology of grace, a love in and beyond death.

If we are to continue to use the language of grace at all in our time, it seems to me we can only do so in the awareness of this destiny and sending and calling where we most bitterly ask the why-question, oppressed and crushed by the obscure mystery of our human existence. Grace shows itself where we break through despair into the affirmation of praise. This is the fundamental experience of grace, neither 'objective' nor 'subjective': it is the passage through ultimate negation into the blessed peace beyond the Cross in the exchange of love of Jesus and the Father, the exchange which Christian tradition has called the Holy Spirit. And it is a passage as real as God and as man, as real as Jesus.

For if we call destiny the *form* of a theology of grace, we may call its *content* transfiguration and transformation. Our destiny, our calling, is to be transformed. 'Lo! I tell you a mystery. We shall not all sleep, but we shall all be changed' (1 Cor 15.51). The Transfiguration of Jesus reported in the synoptic Gospels, expressed as it is in the terminology of Jewish apocalyptic literature, has its counterpart in our own transfiguration, expressed in terminology which is reminiscent of Hellenistic mystery religions: 'And we all, with unveiled face, beholding (or 'mirroring') the glory of the Lord, are being changed into his likeness from one degree of glory into another' (2 Cor 3.18). St John Damascene sums up a Greek theological tradition when after describing the greatness of the human creature, at the boundary between visible and invisible creation, he goes on:

> Here, that is, in the present life, his life is ordered like that of any living thing, but elsewhere, that is, in the age to come, he is changed; and this is the utmost bound of the mystery, he is deified by merely inclining himself to God; becoming deified by participating in the divine radiance, not by being changed into the divine substance (*De Fide Orthodoxa*, 2,12; PG 94,924).

Two points arise for consideration here, in the light

of what was said earlier about the process and praxis of meaning: how shall we understand this transformation, and in what sense is it to be thought of as real? Are we dealing here merely with the metaphors and myths of past worlds, Jewish apocalyptic fantasies or Hellenistic mysteries, or can we relate these metaphors and myths to our own sense of the world? Any serious attempt to answer these questions would take us very far into dark and difficult regions; but we may try to offer the brief sketch of an answer, conscious of the need to continue the Catholic tradition in which grace is consistently seen as a reality.

We spoke earlier of meaning as a process and praxis in which the world to which man belongs becomes the world which belongs to man; and we also drew attention to the way in which our experience of Jesus Christ in faith enlarges the boundaries of the human world of meaning and gives it a new dimension. If we take it for granted that human meaning is merely 'subjective', consisting only of the ideas in our heads, then the experience of Jesus Christ in faith can be regarded similarly as only subjective, at best an addition to our stock of ideas. But if we take seriously the suggestion that meaning is primarily a process and a praxis, then the possibility at least arises that the new sense of meaning disclosed in our experience of Jesus Christ may involve a transformation of our lives as real as, or more real than, any human activity of transforming the world. And if by 'grace' we understand primarily the novelty introduced into our lives in our experience of Jesus Christ, then grace too will be 'real'.

The difficulty here is in great part what we take reflectively or unreflectively as our primary instance or touchstone of the real. As the etymology of the word suggests, by 'real' we commonly understand whatever stands over against us as a 'thing' (Latin res), something independent of our thoughts about it, something 'objectively' there. In the Greek philosophical tradition, to which the Catholic theological tradition for centuries has been the heir, the discussion of the real, of what fully and truly exists, has always taken its departure from the world of nature, whether so as to subordinate it to a world of ideas which are not the product but the source of human understanding and of the world; or by returning to this world as the embodiment of such ideas. Where the 'spiritual' is seen as the ultimately real, it is still with reference to the world of nature that 'spirit' is judged to be *more* real: it is the reality of the natural world that spirit transcends by being more real than nature.

It does not seem to me that we can any longer be at home in this tradition of the understanding of the real, any more than we can be at home in an understanding of the real which sees reality primarily in the world of 'facts' and laws ascertained by nineteenth-century physics. What is suggested here is that we should take as our primary instance of the real what has already been proposed as the primary instance of meaning: the 'genetic moment' in which man is transformed as he transforms his world. By analogy, we may say that budding is more illuminatingly the moment of the real than the flower or the soil out of which it grows: the genetic moment is the prime moment of the real, the moment of truth.

I should like to quote here a description of the 'genetic moment' from a paper written some years ago in which the present writer attempted to show how Christianity identified in the experience of the Spirit of Jesus a universally human awareness of the core and nucleus of the real:

> Every genetic moment is a mystery. It is dawn, discovery, spring, new birth, coming to the light, awakening, transcendence, liberation, ecstasy, bridal consent, gift, forgiveness, reconciliation, revolution, faith, hope, love. It could be said that Christianity is the consecration of the genetic moment, the liv-

ing centre from which it reviews the indefinitely various and shifting perspectives of human experience in history. That, at least, is or ought to be its claim: that it is the power to transform and renew all things: 'Behold, I make all things new' (Apoc 21.5).

What is being said here is that there is a universal experience of the new as constituting the meaning and reality of human life; and that Christianity assumes this universal experience of the new and gives it an uniquely new sense, a potentiated sense of the new, in the radical novelty of the resurrection of Jesus Christ communicated to those who receive him in faith. Christianity reinterprets universal human experience, even the experience of new life, and gives it new meaning and reality. This new Christian experience of the new is not only a private or subjective affair; it is manifested as transformation of the individual life and of the life of the community – the Church; and both these as witnesses to the risen Christ in his Spirit.

The primary sense, then, which we may allow ourselves to pick out in our theological use of 'grace' is just this transcendent novelty disclosed in our lives as the gift of Jesus Christ communicated. It is a novelty which shows itself in many ways: some of these ways we shall look at briefly in the remainder of this book. But as we have tried to suggest, this primary sense of 'grace' has a kind of built-in transcendence; it is open to a God who is infinite not only because he transcends a creation identified as nature or cosmos, or even because he transcends an historical process identified as a prolongation of the past into the future. The transcendence of grace as we should like to understand it is to be seen in its openness to a communion with a God who effortlessly affirms himself as the total answer to our most despairing question 'Why?', as he who transcends the ultimate inarticulate aspirations of our hearts, our quest for meaning: indeed by initiating those aspirations he guides and forces us to acknowledge him as the ever-greater, ever-newer God in Jesus Christ: the Meaning of meaning.

2. The Faces of Grace

(a) *Nature and Grace.*

At the beginning of the last section we alluded briefly to the problems involved in seeing the coming of Jesus Christ as an historical happening which took place within a pre-established natural order. It is certainly part of our ordinary way of looking at things that we ourselves, mankind generally, seem to occupy space and time in the same sort of way as tables and chairs, houses and trees, stars and atoms. The obviousness of this way of looking at things depends on a tacit reduction of this diversity to a single simple type, and it dissolves as soon as we begin to consider the very different ways in which something is 'in a place,' 'at a time.' A plant, still more an animal, lives in an 'environment,' which is not just the sum of physical objects around it but forms an order of significance appropriate to the given organism. The 'world' of the honey-bee differs from the 'world' of the robin. Organic existence offers us a telling instance at a comparatively simple level of the genesis of meaning; historical existence, which is the existence of mankind, displays the genesis of meaning as its proper and distinctive mode.

So even before we begin to consider the special problems involved in the historical happening of Jesus Christ as a unique member of mankind, we need to remind ourselves that history does not simply take place 'within' a neutral nature, and that historical time is only conventionally measured by cosmic clocks, solar or atomic. The 'sense' of nature has to be disclosed in history, where 'place' becomes 'environment', 'context', 'world', and 'time' becomes 'memory', 'hope', 'presence'.

Theologically speaking, Jesus Christ comes as the fulfilment of historical time, the ultimate meaning of memory, hope and presence, the origin of the total environment and context of mankind, the heart of the world. In Jesus Christ nature finds its historical consummation in a unique transcendent novelty. The theological problem of nature and grace consists in how we are to understand 'fulfilment', 'consummation' and novelty in the coming of Jesus Christ, once we have distinguished this problem from the more general problem of the relation of nature and history.

The theological problem is further complicated by the fact that the coming of Jesus Christ is presented in the documents of Christian revelation as a remedy for sin. We may put this in a different way: according to the Christian documents, Jesus Christ came to save sinners; it is only a theological abstraction to consider what the coming of Jesus Christ might have been if there had been no sin. Traditionally, the former formulation has been called Thomist, the latter Scotist. What is certain is that reflection on the significance of the coming of Jesus Christ, and of divine intervention in the history of the Chosen People before him, in fact began with the redemptive work of God, his forgiving and liberating love, and only then considered the universal bearing of this love in the total environment of mankind in space and time: the creation. On the one hand we have to avoid so presenting the mystery of God's redemptive love in Jesus Christ that the coming of Christ is only externally and contingently related to its total environment; on the other, we have to avoid so presenting God's love in Christ that its concrete manifestation in the redemptive death of Jesus is only a further expression – the highest, certainly – of a creative love which we could well have known apart from the death for sin. In the language of grace, we have to avoid seeing the grace of forgiveness as merely a special case of a general divine benevolence; and we have to avoid seeing grace as merely forgiveness.

Finally, we should note that the terms 'creation' (= 'the created world') and 'nature' do not exactly coincide. Setting aside the fact that 'nature' has been understood in very various ways even in the history of Western thought (Aristotle, Spinoza, Wordsworth, the 'natural sciences'), it cannot be said that what God created is simply a neutral nature: at the very least, what God created is precisely *created nature*, that is, an expression of his creative purpose, which cannot be detached by theologians from that purpose and considered in isolation. It is important to bear in mind that 'nature' is not a term of the documents of Christian revelation; there is no Hebrew equivalent in the Old Testament, and the few occurrences of the Greek *physis* in the New Testament cannot in themselves be made to bear any theological weight. 'Nature' entered Christian tradition when theologians began to reflect on revelation with the help of categories drawn from Greek thought, especially Stoicism and later, more systematically, Aristotelianism. To say that the 'nature' theologians are interested in is *created nature* is to recognize that the nature we know might have been otherwise, that it is contingent not only in being finite but also in being the expression of a choice and a purpose, God's will.

What we need to look for in the documents of revelation, then, is some guide to the sense of God's predestining purpose, embracing creation and consummation. We have to learn to see that purpose as working itself out in stages, and hinged, within that containing purpose, on the exercise of created human freedom, above all the human freedom of Jesus Christ. If God's purpose for man is the union of man with God, that union is to be achieved in the free acceptance by man of God's purpose in mutual love.

estiny is the summons and invitation of the God of
ve, that we should respond to him in loving and
eative consent. It is just when we enter by this con-
nt into the mystery of God's love that we discover
r what is always a first time the new meaning of our
es, in a genetic moment.

So the typical moment of freedom is conversion, the
oment of birth into a higher and deeper range and
tensity of meaning, the meaning of our own individ-
l lives within the meaning of the destiny of man-
nd. Destiny is an order of transcendence which has
be traversed in a freely growing and expanding
ve: 'And all shall be well, and all manner of things
all be well.' When we speak of 'conversion', we
dinarily understand turning from one opposite to
other; this is how it is understood in the Bible, as
eturning to God from alienation or culpable forget-
lness. And so the genetic moment of conversion is
rceived as a moment of God's forgiving and liberat-
g grace. As we saw in the previous section, it is by
y of this experience of conversion as forgiveness
d 'justification' that we may begin to understand
plenitude of divine love which does not need to
give in order to fulfil. In Jesus, by a unique con-
action, God's forgiving grace is realized in a free
nsent which can bear the sin of the world because it
s to turn away from no sin of its own: here forgive-
ss shows us the inwardness of pure gift.

The interaction of divine grace and human freedom
s long been found acutely problematic in the history
Christian theology. It is the present writer's view
t the mutual play of divine and human freedom in
consent of love, elicited in a genetic moment in
ich the human freedom awakens to a discovery of
elf in a discovery of the source of its own being,
ers the proper locus of the mystery, prior to all
orts to analyse it. It then becomes possible to see
edom as exercised less in the choice of one alterna-
e among many already given in advance than in

Behold, I am doing a new thing; now it
springs forth, do you not perceive it? (Is
43.19).

Chapters 40-55 of the book of Isaiah offer us perhaps
the most vivid expression in the Bible of the transcendent *novelty* of God's purpose in history. The prophet
is consoling and comforting Israel in exile; and he
exhorts and promises by celebrating the sublime and
sovereign freedom of God's purpose. God is free
Creator and Redeemer at once: the freedom of his
power in creating the world and the freedom of his
power in redeeming his people in the liberation from
Egypt in the past sustain and illuminate each other,
and provide an unshakeable guarantee for the new
exercise of his free creative power in the liberation to
come. The mutual involvement of 'cosmic' and 'historical' creative power shows itself even in the detail
of the metaphor: water, for instance, is water created,
water overcome in the passage of the Israelites, and
water as eschatological renewal in the Spirit:

For I will pour water on the thirsty land . . .
I will pour my Spirit upon your descendants
(44.3).

Creation, redemption and consummation form the
three stages of a single purpose, each stage reflected
in the others, united in the total self-presentation of
the I of Yahweh: 'I, I am Yahweh.' Promise and fulfilment sustain each other.

It is surely no accident that within this sequence of
magnificent poems celebrating God's sovereign power
there also occur the profound meditations on the
humiliation of the Servant of Yahweh, culminating in
chapter 53. The texture of this experience of God's
sovereign and delicately sympathetic power is shot
through with the intense awareness of defeat and
abandonment, personally endured in the figure of the
suffering Servant, and overcome in a moral and
religious transcendence which transfigures the saving
power at work in it. Our experience of God's creative

love would inevitably be trivialized if we did not discover it as the ground of his love in mercy and forgiveness.

It is in this sense that we may say that the Cross is at the centre of creation. 'And I, when I am lifted up from the earth, will draw all men (a well-attested alternative reading has 'all things') to myself (Jn 12.32). Jesus is the Way to the glory of the Father, and his Way is the way of the Cross: his Life and Light are *not overcome* by death and darkness. We cannot even surmise what God's love might have been like without the rebellion of sin unless we discover that love as a love which has overcome sin. So too Paul writes: 'For it is the God who said, "Let light shine out of darkness," who has shone in our hearts to give the light of the knowledge of the glory of God in the face of Christ' (2 Cor 4.6). The genetic moment of God's revelation illuminates beginning and end, creation and consummation. Creation itself is promise fulfilled in Christ. Again Paul couples into unity the statements about the God in whom Abraham believed, 'who gives life to the dead and calls into existence the things that do not exist' (Rom 4.17), and Abraham who was justified by his faith. The genetic moment of our own awakening to faith allows us to discern in its own novelty the transcendent novelty of the God who creates, liberates and fulfils.

It is true that in one sense Christianity surpasses tragedy, where reconciliation to a transcendent order is opened up by the reassertion of that order in the agony of an individual all but overwhelmed by alien and anonymous powers. Christianity offers the fullness of reconciliation as the plenitude of divinity in Christ. But the way to the discovery of that plenitude is still the way of agony, the absoluteness of the affirmation has to be lived into by way of the negation of the Cross. It is only once the transcendent novelty of God's liberating and victoriously forgiving grace has been perceived in Christ that we can rediscover the

freshness and the novelty of God's
'There lives the dearest freshness dee
(Hopkins).

(b) *Grace and freedom.*

God's predestining plan of creatio
mation, it was said, hinged on human f
a single divine initiative which includ
the end, end in the beginning, hur
inserted: human consent to the pur
folds it, or human withdrawal from th
out escape from it. Human freedom i
love by the love which creates, sustain
contracts into a private prison, a solit
can only be experienced as an alien
wrath.

The coming of Jesus Christ is th
pression of God's initiative of grace. F
consent to God's purpose, the resoluti
question of human destiny by a going-
glory of the Father and final consumm
primary consent in freedom to that c
own, his acceptance of the mission of h
initiative of grace for mankind is work
free human consent to his destiny, th
the Father which he makes his own.

What we have above all to understa
the first place and then in ourselves,
destiny for man involves a passage, an
into the depths of God's purpose and s
Human freedom is only properly app
dimension of destiny in which it is tru
the course of our daily lives choices ar
dom; but the fundamental sense of th
only be assessed when they are evalua
our ultimate destiny. Indeed, the cru
those in which our destiny makes some
cisely in virtue of the choice. For desti
imposed on us by some alien and ins

the creation by choice of a new possibility of inward communion. Grace allows freedom to discover in this communion the ever-newer God.

Life as we live it is open-ended. Part of our sense of the open future of our lives emerges only when we reflect upon our past. This kind of reflection has the character of a farewell discourse, where we order the past into a pattern of relevance to an open and obscure future, where death is at once the assumed term of our lives, a question permanently put to our present awareness of ourselves, and an ultimate transition into a beyond. This pattern is both discovered and constructed, in an interplay of circumstance and choice: for circumstances pose the possibilities of choice, and yet by their intrinsic ambiguity await the definition of choice:

> Footfalls echo in the memory
> Down the passage which we did not take
> Towards the door we never opened
> Into the rose-garden
>
> (T. S. Eliot, *Burnt Norton*)

Our selves, what for each of us is 'I', are only partially determinate; what in our past is only latent and hence shut off and fixed in an unconscious, can be brought to light in a choice, perhaps a symbolic gesture, which reintegrates into a whole of realized consciousness. We may perhaps see Purgatory as the realization of the whole self in process of reconstitution in virtue of a definitive choice by and for God's love. Our past, individual and collective, is part of that world to which we belong which we have to make into a world which belongs to us by surrendering it to God.

Freedom in one sense is the power to make the transforming choice; it is also the condition brought about by the choice made, the transformation achieved: 'Love, and do what you will.' Freedom both brings to birth and has to be brought to birth; destiny

83

is the obscure pattern of free choice to be discovered, linking past and future, the answer to the why-question which we both find and make ourselves. If St Augustine's *Confessions* remains the basic document for an experiential reading of the theology of grace and freedom, it is in the novel that we should look for a modern counterpart to Augustine's sense of the shape of his life taken as a whole; for instance Patrick White's *Riders in the Chariot* or *The Vivisector*, or Iris Murdoch's *Bruno's Dream*. The more we expose ourselves to the complexities of human existence, its apparently arbitrary conjunctures, its absurdities, the shifting succession of its partial failures and partial successes, the more urgent becomes the demand for meaning and sense. The mystery of divine grace and human freedom is that there is *always* a creative choice which finds and is found by God's ever-transcendent, ever-new love, the sovereign *mysterion* of his self-giving, its unending spring of life.

When we see a human life as a whole, as having a shape both unique for the individual and typical as an instance of the destiny of Jesus, we may find the best place into which to insert the language of 'merit'. What seems fundamental to the notion of merit is the *continuity* of a human life lived in response to God's predestining purpose. The temporal sequence of a human life involving choice and circumstance acquires its proper sense as *growth* in the order of response and not merely in the biological order of birth, ageing and death. Human beings can grow together into a communion by way of a temporal sequence of mutual successive response; but the growth is not realized in the dimension of time, friendship is real intensively rather than extensively. The Church grows into the fullness of Christ by way of a historical sequence of successive response; but the growth does not take place in the dimension of history, it is realized in the dimension of God's purpose (cf.Ephesians).

The notion of merit implies that successive stages

of growth, in spite of lapses and deviations, form a continuous curve with a definite sense. The successive stages exhibit the continuity of a moral person responding to God's purpose under the impulse of the Spirit. It is not necessary to suppose that this continuity should become a matter of experience, though there is no reason to suppose either that growth in the love of God as a discriminating sympathy with the complex destiny of mankind should not show itself as an enlargement of the heart. One would like to think that awareness of growth is the normal case, but we have to allow for the obscure and mysterious shape of a human destiny, where continuity may only become manifest as the culmination of apparent strayings and absences. The 'economic' metaphor of reward for services rendered may well be regarded as a way of talking about the moral continuity of a human life sustained and guided by the Spirit which no longer proves as helpful as it once seems to have done. But if we believe that it is to a communion of love that God calls us, that we are both called God's children and so we are (1 Jn 3.1), then it must be through a free, creative response of love that we grow in love; and it is to the stages of cumulative growth in this responsive communion that we should refer when we speak of merit.

What 'merit' is drawing attention to, then, if we are to follow the author of 1 John, is that experience – knowledge in faith – of transformation by love which provides the immediate, incontrovertible guarantee and pledge of our initial transformation into the glory of God. '*We know* that we have passed out of death into life, *because* we love the brethren' (1 Jn 3.14). The repeated 'We know' of 1 John evokes the realized gift of God's love which anticipates its consummation in glory.

(c) *Grace and sin.*

Sin is the failure of love. 'By this we know love,

85

that he laid down his life for us; and we ought to lay down our lives for the brethren' (1 Jn 3.16). All that is not love, or is less than love, is sin. If we want to see sin for what it is, we have to look at the crucifixion of love in Jesus, and detect our own collusion in the sin of the world which comes to a head in that crucifixion.

Our human destiny is to enter by our freedom into the freedom of the children of God (Rom 8.21), to be born again, from on high (Jn 3, the discussion with Nicodemus). All that is not reborn and recreated, all that is not assumed into the glory of God, is sin. In this present life we cannot always tell with certainty what is on the side of life and what is for death; but ambiguity is not the same thing as neutrality. Our destiny to be transformed is not an optional extra; it is the common future of mankind, to be evaded only by conscious or unconscious rejection. For Christianity the 'everyday world' is not closed in on itself; when we insist that the everyday world is all there is, then we close this world off from its proper sense in the purpose of God. As we have seen, even 'nature', the created order on its way to its consummation in glory, has continually to be rediscovered.

The primary definition of sin is negation, omission, *aversio a Deo*, turning away from the living God who calls us, a failure of response. This turning away takes shape in a multiplicity of turnings to what is less than God. But it is not the turning to what is less than God which constitutes the sinfulness of sin; we may always turn to God through what is less than God, and in fact ordinarily do so, above all in our human relationships. We find God in our brethren, reject him by rejecting human relationship. Rejections harden into personal and collective systems of alienation, which reproduce themselves and multiply in the succession of generations, in the family and in society at large.

If we speak in this section of the faces of grace, we may contrast them with the masks of sin, personal

86

and collective mystifications, the false persona, the social myth. It is only when we recognize the spuriousness of the masks of sin that we can understand how sin is not a proper alternative to grace, how the idols are 'nothings'. The most profound meditation on sin and love in the New Testament, the First Epistle of John, concludes abruptly, 'Little children, keep yourselves from idols.'

The order of grace, the order of the only ultimately real, is free mutual self-giving, initiated by the free self-giving of the God who is love. It is an order of growth in communion, a continual rebirth and re-discovery of the ever-new preciousness and generosity of the beloved. Wherever there is love, there is an image of God, an image which can become an idol. Sin is the disease, the cancerous growth of love. But if someone has never loved he is wholly 'nothing', he has become his own mask, he has found neither himself nor his brother nor God. 'He who does not love does not know God; for God is love' (1 Jn 4.8).

An older, though not, I believe, a primitive, Christian theology distinguished sharply between sins and 'imperfections', as it distinguished between commandments and counsels. When we recover the sense of a single destiny to transformation with Christ in glory, we recover too the sense of being at once really children of God and those who deceive themselves if they say they have no sin (1 Jn 1.8). We have been really reborn; but that newness of life has to be continually revived in a process of growth punctuated by genetic moments of rediscovery of the sense of the whole, a rebirth in grace into grace.

(d) *Grace and sacraments.*

The liturgy of the Easter Vigil shows a deep understanding of the multiple force of God's creating and consummating love by beginning its readings on the night by the newly-lit paschal candle with the first creation narrative from Genesis. If from this starting-

87

point we allow ourselves to recover the movement of the hymn of praise in Ephesians 1, we may see that the sense of this hymn is the continuity of divine purpose in creation, restoration and consummation: the springing of the grass, the flight of a bird, the drift of the stars, the expansion of the universe, are to be read as the figures of the springing, flight, drift and expansion of a historical process of human meaning which finds its ultimate sense as the praise of a divine purpose of creative love, initiating a communion in a divine and human centre of communion, Jesus Christ. The heart of Jesus is the centre of the world to which man belongs and the world which belongs to man: his is the human heart in which we discover that God is love. So it is in Jesus Christ himself that we may see the unity of creation and recreation, of 'nature' and 'grace'.

For we can only discover the fundamental and underlying continuity of nature and grace in God's plan by surpassing through the death of Jesus the manifest discontinuity in this plan, introduced by the rejection of meaning disclosed as sin. Sin is the manifest discontinuity in the mystery, grace the victorious reintegration into an ultimate continuity and unity, the climax of the mystery. The violence and the desolation of the death of Jesus, the brutal disruption of meaning into blank meaninglessness, are the figure of human negation and alienation, a discord in the nature created by God for transformation into glory: grace is the resolution of the discord into a harmony which is the deep and original purpose of God's love. At least one of the functions of what we ordinarily regard as great art is the rediscovery and affirmation of the unifying sense of human destiny, a joy too deep for tears. Grace is re-discovery of the comprehensive unity of the initiative of God's love, a unity to which we can only penetrate stepwise, by a continual conversion, a dying and rising again with Jesus. So Lear to Cordelia:

We two alone will sing like birds i' the cage:
When thou dost ask me blessing, I'll kneel down,
And ask of thee forgiveness: so we'll live,
And pray, and sing, and tell old tales, and laugh
At gilded butterflies, and hear poor rogues
Talk of court news; and we'll talk with them too,
Who loses and who wins; who's in, who's out;
And take upon's the mystery of things,
As if we were God's spies.

An excellent critic has drawn attention to the importance of the word 'grace' in Shakespeare's later plays. Writing on *The Winter's Tale*, the central theme of which may be said to be 'nature' and 'grace', he writes:

> The play, indeed, contains a profound and highly individual effort to bring the impasse suggested by Shakespeare's exploration of the part played by 'blood' in human experience – a part at once destructive and, potentially, maturing – into relation with feelings which imply the understanding of a positive spiritual conception (Derek Traversi, *Shakespeare: the Last Phase*, p. 119).

The dramatic exploration of a transcendent unity of nature and grace may help us to consider this unity in those figures of divine purpose which we call generically the 'sacraments'. In each sacrament, 'nature' is assumed into a creative purpose which transcends it by being made to bear in a significant action the death and victory of Jesus, his passage into the glory of the Father. Nature, Passion and Glory are integrated into a comprehensive sign. In baptism the unfathomable sea of waters, the abyss, becomes the figure of life, death and new life, the unfathomable fullness of God's love enacted and suffered on the Cross. The Epistle to the Ephesians sees the connexion of man and wife at the beginning – but the beginning is an anticipation of the connexion of Christ and the Church (5.32), for

89

which he 'gave himself up' (v.25). Penance is the sacrament of reconciliation, the figure of human communication restored, the renewal of the human bond in the new head of the human race, the second and last Adam, who reconciles men to each other and to the Father. In each case the ultimate sense of the beginning is rediscovered in a consummation which transcends it, through a figure which bears the death of Jesus. To celebrate the sacraments is to submit to the figure of God's unifying and predestining purpose, to be transfigured in the death of Jesus into glory: to 'take upon's the mystery of things.'

Because, as St Thomas says, the eucharistic action is a consecration, the term of the action is not only the human *behaviour* of eating and drinking, a ritual 'doing'; it is also the *artefact* of human meaning, something ritually 'made'. And it is this which becomes the real presence of God's love in the victorious death of Jesus, the real presence of the Giver in his gift. The new meaning imposed on the human artefact is just as real in terms of things made as the meaning imposed on human actions in terms of things done. What was bread and wine has become the embodiment of God's gracious love in the communicated flesh and blood of Jesus; what was transformed by human labour from the world to which man belonged into the world which belongs to man – wheat into bread, grapes into wine – is now transformed into the world of God's creative love, transfigured flesh and blood.

(e) *Grace and the Spirit.*

Although later tradition speaks frequently of the 'grace of the Holy Spirit', the phrase would make no immediate sense in biblical language, where we might have rather the 'grace of Jesus Christ'. If we were to pick out one dominant characteristic of what is said about the Spirit in the Bible, in both Old and New Testaments, it would seem to be that the Spirit is creative and life-giving. The Spirit is the agent of

God's purpose in creation and transformation; it spans the whole arc of God's creative act from beginning to end and leads the creature back into the depths of the holy mystery of God from which it originally issued. The whole of chapter 8 of the Epistle to the Romans needs to be read in this perspective:

> For the creation waits with eager longing for the revealing of the sons of God . . . We know that the whole creation has been groaning in travail together until now; and not only the creation but we ourselves, who have the first fruits of the Spirit, groan inwardly as we wait for adoption as sons, the redemption of our bodies (vv. 19-23).

The Resurrection of Jesus is the supreme instance of the creative power of the Spirit; it is the revelation of a new meaning of 'life'. As at the beginning it was 'life' which was given by the Spirit, so in the new order of the resurrection it is again 'life' which the Spirit bestows. The shift in the meaning of the word itself indicates the inner order of creation to transformation, 'nature' to 'grace'. There is a continuity of God-given life from creation to transformation, by way of a shift of level and also by way of the discontinuity of sin revealed in the death of Jesus. The life-giving Spirit which transforms us into our predestined glory as sons of God comes to us through the death of Jesus on the Cross and marks us with the same sign of suffering and death: 'provided we suffer with him in order that we may also be glorified with him' (Rom 8.17). Our human destiny to be transformed into glory by the creative power of the Spirit is a crucifixion into a new life. If we are to speak of the 'grace of the Holy Spirit', we must mean first this transformation by which we are drawn with 'unutterable groanings' (Rom 8.26) into the 'depths of God' (1 Cor 2.10), our inward humanity being renewed day by day in affliction and suffering (2 Cor 4.16-17).

The destiny is the unique destiny of each one of us,

and it is also the common destiny of all mankind, typified in the destiny of Jesus. The 'commonness' of this shared destiny appears in the Pauline phrase, 'the communion (or 'fellowship') of the Holy Spirit': it consists in a sharing in the gift of new life bestowed by the Spirit. So the phrase is the final member of the whole blessing: 'The grace of the Lord Jesus Christ and the love of God and the fellowship of the Holy Spirit be with you all' (2 Cor 13.14). The three members of the blessing express a single 'Trinitarian' purpose; the blessing places the Christian community under this purpose for our transformation, God communicating his life so that we might enter into communion with him. The sense of our human destiny is the progressive entry into communion with the God who communicates himself, with the God who is Love. Our understanding of 'grace' is our continuous reawakening to the infinite inequality of divine and human love.

After reaching the end of this attempt to offer a perspective for a theology of grace, a reader may wish to object: 'You have said nothing clear and distinct about grace itself. You have talked about everything else in Christian revelation and under the sun, and kept throwing in the word "grace" pretty well at random. How can you call this a theology of grace?'

The objection would be perfectly fair. I would freely concede that in one sense there is no such thing as a theology of grace, in the sense, that is, that there is a theology of Christ or the sacraments. As was remarked at the end of chapter 1, 'grace' is not one item among the many gifts God has bestowed on man. It was suggested there that 'grace' might turn out to be a second-order word, a way of qualifying the whole of God's self-communication to his creature man as a gift beyond all telling: the transcendent novelty of communion between God and man.

What we have attempted to offer as a theology of

grace is to elicit some kind of centre in experience (the genetic moment of meaning) from which, by a kind of pulse of expansion and contraction, we might refresh our awareness of the whole of human existence under God as *gift*, the gift of created existence ordained in freedom (God's and ours) to the gift of communion in love.

There is no way of defining, in clear and distinct ideas, the quality and mode of human existence as God's gift. What is required is a surrender of one's fixed roots in the ordinary world of everyday, that mode of being-in-the-world which unquestioningly 'takes things as they are'. Wallace Stevens's long poem, 'The Man with the Blue Guitar', begins:

> The man bent over his guitar,
> A shearsman of sorts. The day was green.
>
> They said, "You have a blue guitar,
> You do not play things as they are."
>
> The man replied, "Things as they are
> Are changed upon the blue guitar."
>
> And they said then, "But play, you must,
> A tune beyond us, yet ourselves,
>
> A tune upon the blue guitar
> Of things exactly as they are."

The blue guitar of one period of Picasso's painting becomes here the instrument of poetic transfiguration. There is a need for transcendence ('A tune beyond us'), which yet is not a desire for flight or evasion: a need to discover the possibility of transfiguration of the everyday world ('A tune beyond us, yet ourselves . . . Of things exactly as they are').

If we are to discover the mode of human existence as God's gift, we have to learn to 'let go', so as to receive all as gift; allow the breath of the Spirit to aerate our heart's blood, to liberate us into the freshness and fertility of newly-germinating life. We have to be roused from our dream of reality, and waken to the reality in the dream. 'Behold, I make all things new.'

SUGGESTIONS FOR FURTHER READING

SOURCES

Gregory of Nyssa, *From Glory to Glory*. Texts selected and introduced by Jean Daniélou, tr. and ed. Herbert Musurillo, London (1961)

Address on Religious Instruction. Tr. C. C. Richardson, in *Christology of the Later Fathers*, Library of Christian Classics, London (1954)

Augustine, *Confessions*. Numerous translation, e.g. R. S. Pine-Coffin. Penguin (1961)

Writings against the Pelagians. Tr. Holmes, Wallis, Warfield. Nicene and Post-Nicene Fathers, Vol. V (nineteenth-century translation)

Thomas Aquinas, *The Gospel of Grace*. (Summa Theologiae 1a-2ae. 106-114), tr. and ed. C. Ernst, Blackfriars translation, Vol. 30, London (1972)

John of Damascus, *On the Orthodox Faith*. Tr. Salmond, Nicene and Post-Nicene Fathers, Vol. IX

Eckhart, *Selected Treatises and Sermons*. Tr. and ed. J. M. Clark and J. V. Skinner, London (1958)

Ruysbroek, *The Spiritual Espousals*. Tr. E. Colledge, London (1952)

Pascal, *The Provincial Letters*. Tr. A. S. Krailsheimer, Penguin (1967)

Conciliar documents translated in Rondet (see below) or *The Teaching of the Catholic Church,* ed. K. Rahner, Cork 1967, pp. 370-411.

OTHER BOOKS

Barth, K., *The Epistle to the Romans*. Tr. E. C. Hoskyns Paperback edition (1968)

Bonner, G., *St Augustine of Hippo,* London (1963)

Boyle, R., *Metaphor in Hopkins,* Chapel Hill (1960)

Brown, P., *Augustine of Hippo,* London (1967)

Burnaby, J., *Amor Dei*, London (1938)

Ernst, C., 'World Religions and Christian Theology', *New Blackfriars,* 50 (1969), pp. 693-99 ; 731-36

Fransen, P., *The New Life of Grace*, London (1969)

Lossky, V., *The Mystical Theology of the Eastern Church,* London (1957)

Lubac H. de, *The Mystery of the Supernatural*, London (1967)

Meyendorf, J. *A Study of Gregory Palamas*, London (1964)

Oberman, H., *The Harvest of Medieval Theology*, Cambridge, Mass. (1963)

Rahner, K., *Nature and Grace*, London (1963)
Theological Investigations, I (1961), IV (1965)

Rondet, H., *The Grace of Christ*, Westminster, Maryland (1967)

Rupp, G., *The Righteousness of God, Luther Studies,* London, 1953

Stevens, Wallace, *Collected Poems,* London (1955)

Traversi, D., *Shakespeare: the Last Phase*, London (1969)

Wendel, F., *Calvin*, Paperback edition (1965)

INDEX